A Life Story of

Heritage
and Faith

A Life Story of
Heritage and Faith

VERNON CARRIGAN, MD

ARPress
ILLUMINATING IDEAS
EMPOWERING VOICES

ARPress
45 Dan Road Suite 5
Canton, MA 02021

Hotline: 1(888) 821-0229
Fax: 1(508) 545-7580

Ordering Information:
Quantity sales. Special discounts are available on quantity purchases by corporations, associations, and others. For details, contact the publisher at the address above.

Printed in the United States of America.

ISBN-13:   Softcover   979-8-89330-006-2
                eBook   979-8-89330-008-6
                Hardback   979-8-89330-007-9

Library of Congress Control Number: 2024900482

CONTENTS OF CONTENTS

FOREWORD

I have several purposes for writing:

For myself. To organize my life challenges and accomplishments and to compare them against my life's purpose in using my God-given gifts and abilities to enrich the lives of others. This is my true spiritual north.

For memorializing stories and heritage for my children and grandchildren.

And hopefully, to encourage my readers to pursue a similar life mission of blessing others.

You will read and learn of my agrarian, rural, and godly upbringing and how these have made me who I am and to become deeply fulfilled in my life, and how the oak tree and spring on the farm symbolize these precepts.

My journey and success have been nurtured by God and family and many other friends and teachers for whom I am eternally grateful. I can say this is especially true for my wives, Melynda and Ruth, who have given me so much.

I would never have survived the death of Melynda, my son David, my grandson Daniel, and my own near death and my other son's, Jonathan, near death, the latter in accidents, were it not for this heritage, my faith, and the support and abiding love of others.

I speak of faith and salvation in all their facets and how they have sustained me.

I am a faithful Christian and a medical scientist with an insatiable appetite for knowledge and understanding. When a person loses the desire to learn and grow, they begin to die. I strongly believe faith and science are not mutually exclusive, as many believe, but rather beautifully complementary and synergistic.

Please come with me as I chronicle my humble beginnings through education and ministering to patients, friends, employees, and many others.

You will meet some very interesting people and travel with me on foreign mission trips and hear some very interesting anecdotes.

Let's start in 1955 on our farm on the day and occasion of my first remembrances and self-awareness.

Of Early Awareness and Expectancy

I am now 70 years of age, but I still vividly recall standing in front of our old shabby 19th-century stable on a hot summer morning and thinking, "I am four years old." This is the first memory I possess of self-awareness and concept.

The seeds of God, Adam, my agrarian and family heritage, and my future all lie dormant within me at that moment, virgin and gravid, yet furtive and unknown, but yet existing there to be discovered and awakened precious bit by bit, acted upon and methodically made part of the conscious me. As such is the beauty, wonder, and grandeur of life.

The essence of these seeds and their potential was radiating all around me in the sun's warmth, the birdsong, the beautiful scent of flowers drifting to me on the gentle breeze and then into me through my senses, creating a mysterious sensation of expectancy.

Who and what am I?

Who made me and all this?

What shall I do with all this?

What will I become?

How do I relate to others on the same journey?

I would be remiss if I do not now tell of the two great symbols of God and life that exist on our farm. The first is the majestic white oak tree that lives between the stable and tobacco barn. It is at least 250 years old and thus existed with the local indigenous Indians before white Europeans and others came.

It is over 100 feet tall and 15 feet in circumference at the bottom and 125 feet across its widest canopy. In the summer, it is a verdant green, and in fall , it becomes a giant red, orange specter.

To us, it represents the deep heritage that exists in this place of God, worship, strong relationships, and hard work. The roots are of God, the trunk of the Rinehart family who founded the farm in 1878 and the branches of all who have lived, have worked and have been restored here, including the wonderful ladies of the Bethany House to whom I will introduce you later. In all, seven generations of our family have lived in its shelter and watchful eye.

The other living symbol of God and life is the spring 300– 400 yards below the stable and the tree down in the hollow, also close to the farmhouse, where my grandfather, mother and I were raised.

It gives life year-round and represents the power and sustenance of God and His Spirit in our lives. Indeed, I was metaphorically baptized in this water long before being literally baptized after my salvation.

So, dear reader and fellow explorer, please come and join me as we further travel the paths of my life, which I trust will assist you in your own walk in life.

I offer the following poem, entitled Life - Spring:

LIFE-SPRING

Born to richness of heritage,

Enveloped into the warming love.

Of our dark black, fertile land,

As the daffodils wait,

Inside our earth mother.

For the golden call of Spring eternal,

Growing strong in the shade and strength.

Of mighty white oak fraternal,

Like an acorn called to lofty heights,

Pulled there by ray of sun,

And hand of Heavenly Father.

Whilst nurtured by floods of earthly love,

And bounteous flow of nectar like cold spring water.

Prepared with knowledge,

But not yet soul seared in life's fiery furnace,

Nor yet made wise by the inter-weaving,

Of those opposing threads.

Thus, released into life,

With world and heart to win,

But not quite knowing where to begin.

Both victory and loss,

Sail subtly and violently into life,

As soft spring breeze and tumultuous summer storm,

Taking away and adding to essence and being.

Both heights of joy and fertile mind fed with food of knowledge,

Lift me high and drive me in healing touch for others,

While the sting of black, frigid death,

Repeatedly chills heart and marrow.

Not the same innocent youth leaving the farm,

Forever changed by joy, loss, guilt, and harm.

Even dead to my former self,

And yet raised by God to begin again in a new life cycle,

As dead autumn leaves falling to cold hard ground,

Then to sprout again in new spring found.

Now wisdom hammered in by the strife of life,

Sewn in place by God's sweet grace,

Bridging fault lines and past far horizons doth lead,

Never dreamed of before,

Making that which was to be,

And not yet quite is.

Possible in the sunrise of a new tomorrow.

Or ... perhaps ... not .

Success no longer selfish goal to earn,

But a fountain spout for others,

In their own life race for me to yearn.

Life is meant to live and help others to grow strong,

While only to God does justice and judgment belong.

When to home farm I now return,

The oak is the strong root of God's strength reserved.

While the nectar water,

Is a strong spiritual quench,

As from the spring of Elim for me.

One day soon,

God will call my soul to heaven on the gentle breeze of his voice,

As the leaves of autumn are carried on the wings of the wind to a
place,

Of its choice.

May I be remembered here by my love of God,

And respect of man.

In whose service I used fully every gift from His strong hand,

Leaving behind for others more than I kept for self.

Striding in life in yoke with Christ's pace,

Both living and dying of love, wisdom, and grace!

OF FARM LIFE

I wasn't raised in a village, but on a farm, on which I was mentored and loved by many. Fortunately, I never knew abuse or criticism, except the constructive type.

My parents were in their early forties when I was born and had been married for 20 years. I guess I was more than a minor surprise.

When my mother told her doctor she was pregnant, he opined I was a tumor, to which she retorted, "Well, if it is a tumor, it is sure moving a lot."

Thank goodness he was swayed to deliver me by C-section rather than perform a tumorectomy! Ha!

Momma and Daddy were born prior to 1910 to parents who were born in the early 1880s, thus I was 'raised right' by 19th century values. They lived through WW1, the Great Depression and WW2.

They were devout, appropriately strict, frugal, and loving.

Years later, when I was seeing an elderly neighbor as a patient, she declared after greeting me from the exam table, "Mike, it was the talk of the country when Lois was expecting you!" How could I possibly disagree, but it was very heartwarming.

I was born in 1951 and electricity, telephone, the first tractor and first car all arrived on the farm just before I did.

My grandfather, Carrigan, purchased the second Model T Ford owned in the community. Prior to that, he had carried the mail on the Hickory Point rural route in a horse and buggy. One day, the local country doctor passed my Daddy Jim, and his horse on a hill. The horse spooked and ran away down the hill off the road and under a support wire, spreading the mail all over creation and ripping the top off the buggy.

Walla, a new car!

I clearly remember we had a three-party telephone line with the parties having different rings. Yep, that's how eavesdropping was invented, I reckon.

We canned vegetables, dried fruit on the coal house metal roof, had a milk cow and made apple cider. The young ones drank the cider, and some of the adults and farm hands had a special variety in an old wooden barrel in the shed. I always wondered what the difference was!

We also raised hogs for our meat; nothing better than home grown smoked country ham, fat back bacon or sausage served with eggs fried in lard, all produced on our farm. This diet later proved very supportive for my doctoring business. It would have been immediately fatal if not counterbalanced by hard work.

Oh, I almost forgot my momma's homemade buttermilk biscuits, which my Pappy would pull through a big pool of molasses mixed with butter and then slap in his mouth.

Can you smell and taste it all?

Unfortunately, my grandmother, Rinehart, died of rabbit fever ten years before I was born. My other grandmother, Carrigan, died when I was five but did a great job of grandmotherly spoiling us kids first.

We had two cisterns next to the house and once, when I was asked if we had running water in the house, I replied that we certainly did, as soon as my brother and I would draw it, we not only ran it in but sometimes raced it in. So, we actually had racing water.

Thus, since we did not have true, piped-in water, our toilets, or privies, were located outside year-round, rain or shine, hot or cold and night or day; and occasionally, we shared the facility with various varmints. Skunks were bad enough, but believe me when I say, not nearly as bad as the time when a wasp made a feast of my derriere, injecting venom. Zap again. This is also where I learned to read, in part, by using the old Sears and Roebuck catalog.

We raised about ten acres of tobacco by hand, except for labor provided by mules and the single small tractor. I never did it, but one today can only imagine what it was like to clean off a new field with a grubbing hoe or plow a field with a mule and one horse-drawn turning plow. The plow itself weighed 75 pounds.

It was in the tobacco patch where Mark and I were introduced to cursing (cussin' in the country). A farm hand, CP, who had only an eighth-grade education, somehow possessed a doctorate degree in profanity.

We were using hoes, and he was plowing a small, red, unruly mule, and at the end of a row, he encountered a nest of angry yellow jackets. The mule took off in a gallop across the field, and the plow was hitting the high spots. CP was running along, holding on to the plow line, cursing a blue streak that would have made a sailor blush.

Mark and I looked at each other in disbelief at the rapid advancement of our vocabularies by thirty percent in one minute.

My grandfather, Pappy, loved and dutifully cared for his mules. Some few years after my parents married, my father was assisting Pappy in digging sweet potatoes about a half mile across the hollow from the house. They then filled them into burlap sacks and carried them on their backs to rebury in the barn. My father had the temerity to suggest to Pappy that they hook the mules to the wagon and let them do the work. "Never!" My future Pappy made it very clear that they would never bother his mules for something so simple and easy. I am just glad I wasn't born yet.

You see, the mules and their vigor and health were essential for the health of the farm, and Pappy, with his experience and wisdom, clearly understood.

The biggest farming day of the year was the day we planted the garden. Hands were plowing. My brother, Mark, and I were planting, and my momma directed. My father tried to stay out of the way.

Ripe farm tomatoes were my favorite, and I ate them literally by the gallons. They go well with anything, even molasses.

I vividly remember the day my uncle Russell taught me about the principle of ballast. We cut our own hay for winter feed for our cows and engaged a neighbor on a price-per-bale basis to rake and bale it. Thus, the tighter and heavier the bales, the cheaper the job. My uncle, understanding this economic principle, kept telling the neighbor to make them tighter and tighter, thus heavier and heavier.

When I pleaded with Russell that it was nearly impossible for me, as a 135-pound teenager, to lift and handle a 100 plus pound hay bale, his solution was a very simple matter of counter ballast, "Put these rocks in your back pocket, boy."

Yet again, what could I say to counter such a scientifically astute application as that.

Russell was quite a tale teller. He once announced to me that he was starting on making his second million dollars raising tobacco. When I said that he indeed was not, he quickly retorted that he saw he would never make the first million, so then he had just decided to begin making the second. *Zap!*

I once asked him in a moderate summer drought if it were very dry at his house. "Boy, it's so dry up here that I have to prime the dog so that he can pee!" *Zap* again.

Finally, being completely exasperated at a hand who also worked in slow gear, he opined it takes Jay Buck an hour and a half to watch 60 minutes on Sunday nights.

You see, with all this wisdom and humor floating around, it's a wonder I even needed a formal education. But we will get to education in a later chapter.

THE OAK TREE

Two hundred yards south of and below the farmhouse and toward the river and between the stable and tobacco barn stands what we call 'the oak tree'. It is 15 feet in circumference at its base and its canopy is 125 feet across at its widest; and it reaches well over 100 feet toward heaven. In summer, its leaves are a sea of verdant green and in fall, it becomes a flaming red-orange giant specter.

Our mother related that it changed very little during her lifetime, and indeed, it seemingly has not changed during ours either. Without doubt, it predates western civilization in Montgomery County and thus coexisted here with the local Indians.

For 140 years now, six generations of our family have been born, played, worked, lived, died and now lie in final rest in its shade and under its watchful eye. To us, it represents the strong and rich heritage of hard work and family and religious values which God, in His love and grace, has given unto us. We, the current owners, wish to pass this farm, with its mighty oak and this heritage, on to our posterity (including our Bethany House family) as both a remembrance of the past and as a guide into the future.

OF REACE, BUCK AND OTHERS

Reace and Buck were sharecroppers who moved to our farm just after I was born in 1951. He had been married once before and had one older son, Wardell, aka Bug Eye, whom you will meet briefly, later.

Buck was born in 1901 and she in 1917, and they were married in the early 1940s. Her parents also lived on the farm, and together, they were a surrogate set of parents and grandparents.

Buck was a dry witted practical joker. On one occasion when I was four—a lot seemed to happen that year—my grandfather asked Buck to order him a new pair of brogan work shoes from the Sears and Roebuck catalog. The big day finally came as the package arrived, but Buck had taken the new shoes from the box and replaced them with a pair of his old dirty and completely worn-out shoes.

When my Pappy opened the box, I happened to be present. At first, he was surprised, but then, suspecting the truth, rapidly became angry. The innate diagnostic talent within me immediately awoke, and I quickly announced, "They b'okay, Pappy, they b'okay."

Well, that remark was taken to be so funny for all that the irritation was quickly washed away by gales of laughter. That story has been recounted so many times.

Like our house, neither of their houses had inside plumbing and were heated with wood and coal burning grates. On a cold day, a person would cook on one side and freeze on the other, as the heat did not radiate well. So, to warm properly, one had to turn oneself, as if a rotisserie. In the summertime, the houses were cooled by fans and open windows.

Which reminds me that Reace and Buck loved each other and us very much. He liked to tell when he proposed to Reace that he promised her wood and water, implying he would bring them into the house for her. Then, however, he would quickly add, "Wood on her back and water in her eye!" She would then usually hit him over the head in jest and just laugh.

In fact, in many early 19th century southern houses, the kitchen was in a completely separated area divided by a breezeway to lessen the fire hazard and to keep the house cooler.

They cooked with lard and made lye soap in the black kettle outside and washed the dirty field clothes in boiling water in the same. Reace was a great cook, and I loved her fried apple pies. Her more traditional indigenous southern dishes included baked squirrel, opossum and rabbit, and wild poke green salad. Hey, don't knock it if you haven't tried it.

Summer days were spent almost exclusively going to the tobacco fields to work with them. Raising tobacco was a year around job: plant bedding and preparing the field for planting, transplantation, weeding and plowing, poisoning bugs and worms, pulling out the top of the plants so the remaining leaves would thicken and mature, controlling suckers, harvesting, smoking and finally, stripping off the leaves, bundling them and taking it all to market.

It was all very hard, dirty, and difficult work.

I remember Buck explaining that when we were out of school for Labor Day, it was not a holiday to be taken off for rest or play but to actually labor on, as how else was it thus named. Boy, was I naïve then. Bucketized again!

All of this taught me very valuable lessons, such as setting short term and long-term goals and the value and collegiality of honest work. It seems so many youngsters today miss out on this.

Reace also taught me to read, tie my shoes using a rope and a shoe box, play cards and tell time. When I started the first grade, I was well ahead and ready to go!

We had fun, too, wading in the creek, fishing, and shooting each other with cane guns using ripe dogwood berries. We had many pet dogs and cats, and they were like a part of the families: Blacky, Laddy, Tuffy, Brownie, Spot, Smoky, Tommy, and Skipper.

Santa Claus visited Mark and me at all these places. We loved our trains and cap pistols.

Buck had one problem. He was given to intermittent binges of drinking over the years, but when he reached 60, he developed a deep faith and gave it up all at once and remained sober for the remaining 35 years of his life. When asked how he stopped, he just said he finally realized that he could never drink it all up and would leave some for the next fellow.

After I came back home to practice medicine, Buck became my patient, and when he became bedfast, Reace so very devotedly and lovingly cared for him at an assisted living home. They now rest in peace in the Davidson Graveyard on the farm. Well, they are really in heaven. I guess I'll be there one day where many of my relatives also rest, including one set of great great grandparents.

I have a doctorate degree in medicine and my brother a master's degree in theology, but what was modeled for us and given to us by all these loved ones is so priceless that words cannot describe. When Mark and I attended to the needs of thousands of others over the decades, the spirit of these was our foundation, and largely, the fire in our hearts moving us onward.

Today our farm, the Carrigan-Rinehart Farm, is one of 30 Tennessee Century Farms in Montgomery County. We have preserved it as a permanent green space through a conservation easement with The Land Trust for Tennessee.

I am also happy to acknowledge in June of this year, I will be buying back the 220 acres of the farm my father was forced to sell 50 years ago, making 355 acres of green space and wild animal sanctuary. Thus, we hope to preserve our rich, godly heritage for our posterity, both family, other loved ones, and our community.

My father had an uncle, Will Bearden, who lived to be 102 years old. He was born in the early 1880s, and his mother lived in the Hickory Point community as a little girl. Will told the story that during the Civil War Union, soldiers came into the house one night and had his mother's mother prepare a meal for them.

Others kept the little girl in the front room and asked her to sing them a song. Will asked me to guess what she sang to which I replied, "Dixie?"

"Heck no," he said. She sang, 'Who came in while I was gone, but a damned 'ole Yankee with a blue coat on!'

Well, I guess we can assume they didn't get too mad, or I would not be here writing to you now. Ha!

By the way, Will's grandmother's great grandfather, Thomas Weakly, fought in Virginia in the Revolutionary War, qualifying me to be in the Sons of the American Revolution, which I count as a high honor.

I also want to tell you a bit about my aunt Alberta, Russell's wife. She cooked the best chocolate pies ever made, and more importantly, she, when I was but a child, taught me my first words in Latin, 'aqua' and 'agricola'. She was a special person in my life, and you'll see why the Latin was important in the later chapter.

OF COMMUNITY

As previously noted, I was born and raised on a farm in Fredonia/ Hickory Point, TN, which has been in my family since 1878. My parents and extended family instilled in me a sense of faith, hard work and respect for all men: male/female, black/white, ignorant/ educated and rich/poor. I guess when we sang in Bible School that Jesus loves all His little children; I took it literally.

Out there, we were all farmers and relatively money poor, and even though the schools were segregated, all the children played together daily, and all the adults were all our parents. Occasionally, the two little churches even exchanged preachers.

Some of my childhood friends and I stay in touch and others not so much as life goes on.

The two most memorable local events in our history—other than being captured in the Civil War—was the day that the government engineers exploded Lock B dam and lock to smithereens and simultaneously killed a gazillion fish. We all had good fish for free for weeks.

Most of the prime brewed local TN sipping whiskey—aka moonshine or shine or white lightning—was made by CM. If you think the ground fiercely shook the day the dam died, that was nothing compared to the day the revenuers blew up CM's still. It was the talk of the country for years and is now officially a part of our unofficial folklore. No one, to this day, has pleaded guilty or been convicted of any crime.

I digress to take a brief rest from hard remembering. Years later, in downtown Fredonia, there was BJP's garage and card playing station. Their motto was, "Drive 'em in and pull 'em out!" My wife had her oil changed there one day, which went well. She, however, being a city slicker, just could not fathom why in heaven's name, or anyone's name, BJ kept the sandwiches and beer in the same cooler as the fishing worms. I opined why not; it takes less electricity and less room. She still did not quite understand.

After I returned as a doctor, I enjoyed playing cards with my father and friends at BJ's place. There was always a lot of spitting and tall tale telling. In fact, there was no telling what might be told, and I don't mean the weather, either.

When bush hogging on our farm, BJ had to rescue me many times with his wrecker, when I would get the farm tractor stuck. Once, I even suspended it on a stump, all four tires off the ground, hidden in the weeds.

Doc, "How in the world did you do this?!"

"Now how in the world would I know, BJ? I wasn't looking!"

Once, I drove the tractor all the way to BJ's place to have several things repaired, or more accurately, fixed. BJ summoned me to come back and get it a couple of weeks later. Bug Eye was there, too, and when we had swapped a couple of tales, I asked if he had finished everything. Pulling his old cap off his head and replacing it as he was wonton to do when he was thinking or making a point said, "Yea, Doc. I did."

Upon noticing that the choke cable was still loose, I said, "BJ, what about this cable?"

He moved his cap up and down twice now for double emphasis, "Well, Doc, all you got to do is ..."

Bug Eye suddenly butts in, "No, BJ, Doc ain't no tractor-doctor, he's a doctor-doctor!" Gales of laughter. I would describe how BE laughed, but there are not enough adjectives in English to accomplish that.

BE lived a hard life, drank, and caroused, but he was one of us and the son of my beloved RD and BD. They all rest in peace in the Davidson Cemetery on our farm now. I know with confidence that they are all really with God in heaven now because one night, when the time was right, I witnessed to BE, and he accepted Jesus as his Savior. He did not live much longer after that, at least as we understand it here on this physical earth.

Well, getting back to my original story, I ran into CN, a black friend whose father and my father were good friends. His father, LN, made the best BBQ anywhere around the local parts when I was growing up. He runs the county trash station at Fredonia. I asked him to say hello to his sister, BN.

Today, I ran into him again and one of his friends, CM, who were chatting. We are all in our early seventies now. I said hello and CM asked me my name. Upon my telling him, he grinned and said he knew my granddaddy, Carrigan, and my father, T.

He then reminded me that CM, of moonshine still fame, was his grandfather. We remembered and discussed the great explosions of local fame and laughed again.

I then related that my uncle, HC, had been caught making whiskey in my other uncle's barn and spent some time in the local calaboose. "Oh, yes," CM retorted, "your uncle and my grand pappy used to do business together." Now I wonder what that might have been?

CN, "CM and I are cousins."

Doc, "I believe all of us from out here are related, ain't we?"

CN and CM, smiling, "We sure are, we sure are."

Doc, smiling, "And we always got along good, didn't we?"

More smiles. "We sure did. We sure did."

Just after writing this, I encountered CN again and gave him condolences over his sister's passing.

"CN, did you get to tell her I said hello before she died?"

"Yes, I did," he said, smiling softly. "Yes, I did."

"Very good." I softly patted him on the shoulder.

So, you see, one of life's greatest gifts, both to give and receive, is the sharing of the essence of life and faith that has been distilled and instilled into our lives by the love and grace of others with whom we share this precious life.

At the end of Chapter 21, 'Of Diversity', you will find a letter entitled, 'A Better Way', in which I support CRT. I shared it today with one of my childhood friends, KM, referenced above, and here I share his response:

"Beautifully spoken, words so very true. Everyone in my family speaks so highly of you and wishes you were still a doctor. You have created a legacy untouched. I wish more people could have grown up the way we did, with respect for everyone. It's so hard on me trying to teach my grandchildren the proper and respectful way to act when police officers pull them over. They're not doing anything criminal, just being who they are. I highly support the CRT because it's a part of history. I always say I love the way we are still a band of true brothers. Color was never a factor with us."

Believe me when I say these are the words that touch my heart most of all in this book.

PS: I almost forgot to tell the story of the shallow pond on the property adjacent to the house where we currently live. I did not want our boys down there, so I concocted a yarn about a pond monster living there who might catch and eat them. Well, of course it worked as long as needed, and I had borrowed the strategy from my mother, who did not want us to go upstairs at the farmhouse when we were small and rummaging through her things. She said a soap man lived there who would catch us and would make us into soap. It worked, as I didn't go up there until I was ten. But I didn't escape from the baby pen until I was three either, and shown by my brother.

Back to my point. When our boys were about three and six years old, we encountered Jay Buck at the country store one day. Neither Ruth nor the kids had met him before, and unfortunately, he had lost his left forearm in an accident years before.

He approached the car and greeted me, and I introduced him to Ruth. The boys were strangely quiet, and when we moved on, Jonathan, the younger, inquired about the amputation. I just replied he had encountered the pond monster a few years before and had lost.

I know that was bad, but better than drowning in the pond.

I offer this poem written for my Bethany House daughter, Jessie, demonstrating community in the context of God:

Gentle Morning Rain

As dawn breaks low,

Through night's dark shroud.

First, a gentle brush of pink,

Then a rush of orange on gold,

Flowing as a river ribbon

Washing warmth into my soul.

Anon gentle breeze,

Thickens the clouds.

The songbirds stop singing,

To listen and smell the rich,

Life giving rain breach,

The ramparts of heaven.

It slowly descends, begins;
Ping, pang, ping.
Harder and harder,
Now louder and louder,
Nature pauses to drink,
Into its thirsty breast;
Wetter and wetter; richer and richer.

I imbibe its richness,
Into my own heart,
Carried there by a ghost-like ship,
Of misty white fog.

On this special Father's Day,
I somehow feel on that foreign ship,
Dwell, my departed loved ones,
Who've gone away,
Sent by God on rising swell,
To bring peace in midst of soulish swale.

And then just now for good measure,
He paints this rainbow,
From my daughter.
Jess, you see,

On the cords of my heart,

Where there it plays a sweet melody:

"When I lost my Daddy, I thought I would forever have to live this life alone and learn and grow on my own. Left to figure things out on my own! But then, God gave me you and Mom! Dad, I don't tell you this enough, but I am truly grateful for you! I literally think of you as my dad and I stand in awe every day of the grace and love God has shown us by bringing us all together! Happy Father's Day to a man who is faithful to God, loves His people, shares his love with those who need it, and is a remarkable example of restoration! I hope it's a beautiful day for you, Dad! A day that is as beautiful as all the days you have given to me at your farm!"

The rain falls on.

Ping, pang, ping.

God's love and mercy,

As new every morning,

Life giving, sustaining, restoring.

Ping, pang, ping.

Mike Carrigan

6-21-2020

Jessie's Response:

"Tears fill my eyes! Truly, this is a beautiful poem! I was reading In Genesis this morning and of the covenant God made to His people with the gift of a Rainbow! So perfect is His Holy Spirit and I strive to obey the gentle nudge of His calling! You needed to hear that, and I needed to say it! The rain of life always brings a rainbow because our God is faithful!!"

Of Elementary Education

My adoptive sister, Ruth Ann, who is ten years older than me, was the very first person in our lineage to receive a high school education. Many of them were surely significantly intelligent, but they were entrapped in a web of relative ignorance by lack of funds, transportation, and the necessity to work for their sustenance.

Some were frankly illiterate, while others were not.

Maybe that simpler life, without instant communication and worldwide travel, allowed them to be more relaxed and happier.

I, first, and then my brother, was the first to receive college degrees, even advanced degrees, as previously noted.

For me, an advanced education opened so many vistas of knowledge and understanding of the world and God and opportunities for advancement. It becomes no less for the individual than what the Renaissance and Age of Enlightenment did for western culture.

My great grandfather Rinehart was illiterate, but he was not only capable of buying our farm, he also had the means to loan his neighbors money. It was done on a handshake, without a mortgage, and at reasonable interest.

He apparently valued education as he sent my grandfather, Alonzo, aka Pappy, to an academy 30 miles away in Cumberland City. There, he learned the three Rs: reading, writing, and arithmetic. This would have been in the mid-1890s.

As the story goes, once, when he was home from the academy, a neighbor came to make a loan payment; and the father, Jake, asked his son to use his newly developed skills to determine the interest due. Pappy started his calculation, but apparently was taking too much time, which frustrated his father. At this point, Jake used his mathematical intuition and did it himself by arranging pebbles in the yard, apparently forming a primitive abacus.

Certainly, Jake could have been a banker if given the opportunity, but I believe he was happy and fulfilled being a farmer.

My parents, Lois and Vernon, aka T, lived close to each other and about 1–2 miles respectively from the Hickory Point Grammar School, which they attended through the eighth grade.

It had one room and one teacher for all eight grades: What an undertaking! She thus allowed my father, who was apparently gifted in mathematics, to teach the younger children arithmetic.

To have attended high school, they would have had to have walked at least a mile further each way to catch the train into Clarksville. An impossibility, so they never had the opportunity.

My father was a great debater and loved politics; and besides farming, he sold insurance, working with the Tennessee Revenue Department collecting delinquent sales taxes from businesses. He was also elected to represent our district on the Montgomery County Commission.

Certainly, my father could have been a great attorney and politician had he had the opportunity.

As an aside, my parents were childhood sweethearts, and when attending school devised a system on the path to school so that he could easily discern if she had already gone on before him or not. Guess who took great pleasure in mixing up and disrupting the signal. You guessed it, my prankster uncle, Russell. The joys of life were simple then.

I still vividly remember my first day of school at age six at Fredonia. It was a four room, four teacher school for eight grades, with about 120 students. For the first week, we were encouraged to go home at noon, and when my father was late in picking me up, I just knew I would have to spend the rest of my life alone in Fredonia. I warmly remember all my teachers there, and I really feel I got a great beginning in education.

The separation process had begun; seventeen years later, the same process was advanced further when I left the home of my parents to attend medical school in Memphis.

I learned, in addition to the official curriculum, how to play baseball and basketball. In fact, I played basketball with PHS, a most famous UT women's basketball coach, and her brothers. Our little school won the county girls' championship and finished second in the boys' tournament in my seventh grade before we were merged into another school the next year.

I excelled academically but could not spell a whit. Once in the third grade, the word on the spelling test was shut, and I spelled it sh-t. Don't you know Ms. W. had quite a laugh at that one!

In the fifth grade, I got my first spanking for accidentally kicking a girl while I was jumping over a chair. The same teacher later apprehended me for shooting wet paper wads onto the ceiling with a small rubber hose used for dispensing milk. She shook me so hard, it turned my milk into butter.

Finally, on my last day at Fredonia, I refused to allow two friends to copy answers from my final exam paper. What followed was a wrestling match with one of them in the poison ivy patch in the adjacent woods. I was afflicted from head to toe and have never been so miserable in all my life. I finally was cured with a steroid shot. So much for doing the right thing.

I also received two limb spankings that year for minor disruptions called 'fights' and the next year for similar activity. Both those great teachers later became my patients, and we enjoyed laughing about their whipping me and shared the memories with my staff. You know, I took great guffaw over that!

I think this is a good place for a break as I start to talk about high school, but I trust we are already beginning to discover that education is more than memorization of facts and even beyond learning to think critically and goes to the heart of discovering God and in doing one's part in managing His creation in relationship with others.

As a serendipitous example at midnight here, I just now, by email and phone, introduced my longtime friend in China, Dr. Joseph, to a leading thoracic surgery oncologist in Nashville. They are both leaders in their field in the treatment of lung cancer. I trust they will form a meaningful relationship.

Oh, how far we have come.

But for now, I'll see you in high school tomorrow!

PS: I have been thrilled to be involved in refurbishing the old Fredonia schoolhouse into a local park, museum, and meeting house, which we opened last year. So many amazing memories.

Additionally, Dr. Macon's old two room medical office will be moved from across the road, remodeled and added the park. We have many of his books and some of his equipment, which is a miracle as he retired 60 years ago. I barely knew him, but I consider myself akin to him.

OF HIGH SCHOOL AND COLLEGE

At the tender age of 14, I started the daily trek on the bus to Clarksville High School. I was already apprehensive waiting in the gym with all my new classmates for home rooms to be called out.

Principal, "Next class, girls PE."

First name called, "Verna Michelle Carrigan."

It took a few seconds to realize that this name suddenly and without my input and approval had now become my new and official school name.

So, I had to stand, say that I was present and proceed to the girls' PE coach. Gales of laughter. The teacher, let's just say, was less than enthusiastic about my being in her class. She didn't even invite me in to view the facilities, but sent me directly to the office.

I was later notified I had set a new CHS record from time of entry to school until being sent to the office. Perhaps even a Guinness record.

Oh well, I survived and excelled in HS. At the end of eighth grade, the guidance counselors suggested, based on aptitude tests and grades, that I should become a doctor. That's what I strongly desired anyway within myself, and it had already been confirmed by Buck many times and years before.

I didn't want to hurt their feelings, so I just politely smiled, assenting and allowing them to think they had a great idea.

But at least one of the greatest opportunities in my life came out of this when they told me I must take four years of Latin in HS. I must admit the first six weeks were difficult, but then something clicked and thereafter, I excelled, and at graduation, four years later, was selected as the outstanding graduate in Latin.

More important, however, was that I became a student of MTP, the matriarchal Latin teacher in Tennessee and one of the best in the country.

Without doubt, she was and still is, my favorite teacher of my entire life. She not only taught me the principles of Latin but taught and instilled in me the strong belief I could become a physician or anything else I aspired to be.

A priceless gift.

Our school excelled both in state and national Latin contests. I comprehensively studied Roman history during those years and won two national first place finishes. Studying the function of Rome in its evolution from a small city-state kingdom to a republic and ultimately to empire, decay, collapse, and fall taught me more about civics, culture, government, and the motives that drive people and governments than I would have ever learned in formal classes. I thoroughly loved it and still do very much to this day.

Horatius Cocles defending the bridge against the invading Etruscans.

Cincinnatus leaving his plow to govern in a crisis and then laying power aside and returning to the farm.

Julius Caesar and his conquests, writings, and statesmanship.

Augustus Caesar ending a century of civil war existing within the polarized culture and government and ushering in the 200-year long Pax Romana.

Trajan, Hadrian, Antonius, Marcus Aurelius, and Constantine's reinventing the empire throughout several iterations of revival.

The relationship of Christianity to the empire and its spread in the west by conquering the invading conquers with religion.

Ultimately, the emergence of Scholasticism, feudalism, the Holy Roman Empire, Reformation, nationalism, the Renaissance, and the Enlightenment and what they mean for us today.

There are certainly too many similarities, parallels, and lessons to be learned to enumerate here, except to say again how much it has enriched my life. I am so thankful.

As you will learn later, my first wife, Melynda, was killed in an automobile accident on April 22, 1987. My beloved MTP died on the same morning. Even though I was in deep shock and mourning for the loss of my wife, I was late getting to her wake two mornings later, because I just had to go to MTP's first.

Another gift at CHS was during my time there, integration was slowly beginning. I, of course, had no idea of the turmoil or significance of it, but in retrospect, being involved with integration's beginnings was a life enhancing experience that has also enhanced my life significantly.

When I matriculated into Austin Peay State University in the Fall of 1969, my experiences, opportunities, and growing world vision were already drawing me away from the farm. The process would develop an insatiable appetite for more knowledge, learning about people in other cultures and meeting and befriending people in them.

I was now formally a premed student, and I put my mind to it. I majored in both Chemistry and Biology and again excelled, and commuted from home.

I had a four hour per week work scholarship; thus, I paid nothing to go to college and a legitimate Vietnam draft deferment by being in school. A precious gift from LBJ's Great Society.

Gas was only 25 cents per gallon, so my father gave me five dollars per week for gas and five dollars per week spending money.

Don't think for a minute, however, that I was a nerdy bookworm, as I spent several hours per week in the student center excelling in ping-pong, foosball, and various card games, including poker. I usually at least doubled my spending money. Now you know about my only skeletons!

It was during this time my best friend, JJ, and I learned our lifelong hobby of duplicate bridge. We placed in a local game the first time we played competitively on the same day we learned the rules. We are both now long time Life Masters.

I made many lifelong friends with my professors while at APSU, and many became my patients later, which was rewarding for both parties. They never knew, however, about my third major in student center 'studies'.

When Ruth, later my wife and then sister-in-law, was taking general chemistry, she and a professor had a brief discussion of me in which she offered the extracurricular activities. He was flabbergasted and finally asked, "Are we speaking about the same Mike Carrigan here?"

Simple answer, "Yes."

While at AP, I certainly was very well prepared for medical school academically, but also had a good start in forming meaningful lifelong relationships. But it was still very difficult to leave home for Memphis and med school in 1974.

Relative to education, I have already shared it is much more than learning facts or even learning to think critically. At its core, education goes further in becoming a part of the learner and forever changing who they become as an individual in their essence and how they relate to others.

I think this concept might be summarized best by my son, David's treatise on numbers as a junior in HS. It was an English class assignment in describing in 100 words or less what academics meant to him.

"Numbers can dance. I discovered the dance while preparing for the state math contest in geometry. Although the dance starts chaotically with unwieldy problems, order descends as the values interact and force themselves into patterns that settle into place.

New quantities and rules emerge, enhancing the dance and making it more elaborate. After viewing the dance, I now choreograph it. Adding new rules and problems, I watch the dancers create new patterns and I discover the dance's fundamental nature. These discoveries draw me deeper into the dance's engaging beat. I delight in the dance."

Like I said, a great and insightful explanation of knowledge and education.

OF KNOWLEDGE

Let's take an interlude to delve deeper into my ideas on knowledge.

I have concluded that a man's spiritual, relational, secular, cultural, political and scientific beliefs can be represented by three concentric spheres.

Thus, the innermost and smallest sphere represents one's core, foundational beliefs, which in the individual areas are unique in the substance, in the way they interface and their relative weight of importance. The innermost part of this core forms our permanent and immutable values, while the outer part is subject to change as we grow in knowledge as individuals.

The second sphere, which is larger than the first, totally contains the first and represents the sum of all knowledge held by the individual. Note: There is an interface on the periphery of the first sphere where one's newly found knowledge intersects with and continuously challenges our core beliefs. A healthy and growing person is thus constantly willing to reevaluate core beliefs as his knowledge grows.

The first two spheres reside within a third one, which is the infinity of all available knowledge. The surface of the second sphere interfaces with the third, where what we know borders what we don't know. Further note that as the radius of the second sphere of what we know increases, the surface of the interface with the unknown grows exponentially.

Thus, as individual or collective knowledge vastly increases, our ability to look over into the unknown with theory and experiment facilitates the growing and expansion of further knowledge, which then exponentially forces reevaluation of core beliefs.

I would finally posit that the boundary of the infinite third sphere intersects with the mind of God and, thus, all knowledge.

In glory, God will collapse His mind and knowledge through the other layers, and we will finally know as we are known, omniscience.

In the meantime, He has given us His Holy Spirit to lead us into all truth. It is a lifelong process of growing and learning and becoming more like God. In the spiritual realm, this process we call sanctification.

This life, in all its aspects, involves learning and growth, preparing us for glory and eternity.

We all approach this process differently in our uniqueness, but we must be willing to engage in it or else we have begun to wither and die.

Thus, knowledge does not replace faith but augments and complements it in understanding God and His creation.

OF FAITH

As I write this, I'm sitting here in Hickory Point UMC, on its 125th anniversary, listening to a great blue grass band play gospel music. I am carried on the wondrous wings of its notes into the memories of my boyhood.

From my mother and here in the sanctum of this building, I first heard of sin, God and His love, mercy and grace and the forgiveness and eternal life found in Jesus Christ.

Where the band is sitting and playing is the same where we as children sang, led by Ms. ZH our teacher, to our Lord, off key I'm sure, songs such as 'God Loves All the Little Children' and 'Come Into My Heart, Lord Jesus' and 'This Is My Father's World'.

Two sets of my great grandparents, Rinehart, and Bearden, were among the four founding families. My great-great-grandfather David Rinehart was first on the rolls. Were my son, Jonathan and his wife, Randi, and son, Samuel, here today, Samuel would be the seventh generation in our family to worship God and fellowship in this place. They will soon as they are to move here.

When I was thirteen, my mother told me of the need for and the nature of salvation, and I learned the same in confirmation classes at this church. Thus, while all alone in the blackberry patch close to the house on the farm, I accepted Jesus into my heart as my Lord and

Savior. I could not then, nor can I fully explain it now, but it was real and marvelous. It changed my life and set its course.

My faith has sustained me through all the good times and tragedies throughout my life. The experience was repeated on April 3, 2006. It went thus:

"It is a beautiful spring morning, and I was enjoying it on the way to the hospital. I finally arrived in a totally different way from which I had begun … by ambulance and thence by helicopter to a level one trauma center.

"Quickly glancing over at a fallen cedar tree fallen by the furry of a storm the night before …

BAM! *A jolting, jarring explosion …*

"Sitting there alone, stunned, semiconscious, I peer over the front of my SUV. There's a wreck, and I'm in it. Continuing to process, I think I am not going to work today. Feeling multiple broken bones and shortness of breath, I finally consider that I may not go to work for several days, in fact maybe never again.

"Then the big, bad thought, as I remember how my wife, Melynda, had died in a similar accident almost twenty years before, only two miles away on the same highway, finally enters my reality. These may be my last moments in this life. I am immediately consumed by a shroud of deep, black and frigidly cold fear.

"Immediately, the 23rd Psalm plays in my mind by the Holy Spirit: 'Yea though I walk through the valley of the shadow of death, I will fear no evil for Thou art with me. You leadeth me by the still waters and have me to lie down in green pastures. Thy rod and thy staff comfort me.'; feeling better now.

"Then, in my mind's eye, I see Jesus seated at the right hand of the Father, forever interceding for me; peace coming.

"Finally, union comes with the Father as with Isaiah in the temple. I realize it makes no difference at all if I live or die physically, as I am in God's hands.

"Perfect peace replaces feral fear."

I believed then and now that when my time to die does come, I will have that same real peace as will you, my dear reader.

In that brief moment, I realized that my relationship with my God was perfect. All my abilities and talents, family, friends, church and yes, even my earthly toils and interpersonal strife and sins were all totally meaningless. I and my life, the good and bad, became nothing in that wonderful moment, and He became perfectly everything. He already was and is; I just had not really known it until then.

I guess that was the Isaiah moment of my life. Part of me wants to stay there in that moment in time in the temple with God, and in His time, in heaven, that will be the case forever. But for now, God is calling me, us, to heal our relationships with each other and to lead our world in doing the same. Only then will we become His salt and life for our community and the world and nothing else will then seem to matter anymore.

Thus God, we know by faith, is always there to sustain us in this vaporous, transient life, the trials of which serve to make us ever more like our Lord. Even when we lose the most precious people in our lives, the temporal possessions of our lives, or others attempt to steal our dignity or even in facing persecution or death, and thus find ourselves in life's deepest poverty and valleys, we can still, by the power and love of the Holy Spirit and the blood of Christ, receive the richness of the Father into our hearts and share it with others.

Nay, I would go so far as to say that poverty of the heart even facilitates God's using us to give His richness and blessings to others and for others in the same state to receive them. This pattern of living prepares us for our lives in unimaginable glory, where we shall live forever in the heart of God as the body and bride of His beloved Son.

If we really believe these things, the pain and suffering of today, even though real and present and pressing, seem to be seen and lived in with a new purpose as we present our lives in sacrifice as a pleasing aroma to God on His throne in heaven.

Faith, aided by prayer, unlocks the mysteries of God in our lives.

It is the beginning and end of our Christian walk.

For me, in all my life trials, the concept of hupomone—the Greek word for sustaining endurance or patience—has come to define faith.

This has become my rock.

It was Paul's rock ...

This pattern of living prepares us for our lives in unimaginable glory, where we shall live forever in the heart of God as the body and bride of His beloved Son.

I thank each of you for sharing life's trials and joys together with me.

Paul- 2 Cor. 6:1-10:

"We then, as workers together with Him, also plead with you not to receive the grace of God in vain. For He says: "In an acceptable time I have heard you, and in the day of salvation I have helped you." Behold, now is the accepted time; behold, now is the day of salvation.

We give no offense to anything, so that our ministry may not be blamed. But in all things we commend ourselves as ministers of God: in much patience (hupomone), in tribulations, needs, distresses, stripes, imprisonments, tumults, labors, sleeplessness, fastings; by purity, knowledge, long suffering, kindness, by the Holy Spirit, sincere love, the word of truth, the power of God, the armor of righteousness on the right hand and on the left, by honor and dishonor, by evil report and good report; as deceivers, and yet true; as unknown, and yet well known; as dying, and behold we live; as chastened, and yet not killed; as sorrowful, yet always rejoicing; as poor, yet making many rich; as having nothing, and yet possessing all things."

This kind of endurance can apply to any life trial, and it is a supernatural gift of the Holy Spirit.

PS:

A poem telling of the need for faith all the days of our lives:

LEAVES AND LIFE

New England in autumn,

Land bathed in tides of Sun.

Spinning golden strands,

Of lattice red leaves,

Falling to cold, hard ground to be undone.

Trees ever changing;

Leaves ever falling.

Infinite beauty unleashed,

As fiery cannon blast,

Endlessly echoing its note,

Through virgin, woody vale.

But Winter awaits,

Claiming the leaves of fall,

Into its icicle chamber of death,

There to silently sleep.

Under a warm blanket of snow,

Hinging hope on the wings of fate,

Of life again tomorrow.

Trees ever changing;

Leaves ever falling.

Spring arrives,

On the heels of Mercury.

With message from the gods:

The earth from splendid sleep,

Is to arise with great glee!

New green buds doth sprout,

With herald of new leaves,

Proclaiming a great shout!

Trees ever changing;

Leaves ever springing.

Finally, summer rolls in,

As a mighty lion roaring in din.

Trees now with mighty mane of green leaves,

Produce fruit on trees anew,

As the rising Phoenix from ash of its own debris.

But soon to fall again

In new life cycle to begin.

Trees ever changing;

Leaves ever being.

Is it not the same for us,

In which cycles do we trust,

The youthful yearning of spring,

The vigorous valor of summer,

The golden glory of our Fall?

The hoary cold hairs of Winter

Followed by the final chill of death,

But surely also by the hope

Of our progeny purloined.

Trees ever changing;

Leaves ever falling;

Men ever living and dying;

With cycles ever renewing,

With new life again ever bringing and sustaining.

Of Science and Theology in Understanding God and His Creation

In the last two chapters, we have explored knowledge or science in one sense and faith separately. I did this out of expediency, not because they are exclusive of each other, as many believe. Let's take a closer look at their synergy in understanding God.

The pre-Victorian romance poets, Shelley, and Wordsworth viewed nature as mysterious, beautiful and sublime, not to be understood by man in its structure or function and, most especially, purpose. Nature and its beauty, they thought, were to be enjoyed without analysis.

Likewise, Paul wrote in Romans chapter 1 that we should know the invisible nature of things of God by viewing the visible (wondrous and beautiful) things of his creation. Some believe that the explanation and understanding of the structure and function of the creation undermines and diminishes the wonder and sublimity of it. I will try to explain why exactly the opposite is true.

For example, does the understanding of the formation of a rainbow by the refraction of light by water droplets serving as a prism detract or diminish the beauty and wonder of it, and especially of God's promise? Of course not.

Today, astrophysicists and nuclear physicists are pondering answers to man's deepest seeded questions as to where we came from and what is our purpose in the vast cosmos. From where did the cosmos emanate and if from a Big Bang, from where did the seminal singularity of it emanate?

In a parallel fashion, theologians consider the same questions, and ponder the answers, at least in part, to be present in the Bible and other religious texts. Indeed, many see science and theology to be at odds, if not mutually exclusive. I differ in my opinion, as I see the advancement of the understanding of the universe as corroborative for a creation by a well-meaning being, God.

Consider the following illustration in the radii and surface areas of a BB pellet, baseball and basketball. The respective radii in sequence are approximately 2.3, 37.4 and 370mm. The corresponding surface areas thus increase from 66.5 square mm to 17,577 square mm to 1,720,000 square mm!

Now consider the finite BB, baseball and basketball within the relative infinity of the universe. The volume of each illustrative sphere represents our slowing increasing knowledge of the cosmos or creation, if you will. The surface of the spheres represents the interface of our knowledge with the utter unknown beyond which is itself an area, which we cannot even begin to frame much less answer questions about. Just look at what happens to the interface of the known with the unknown, that place where we should have enough insight to pose and solve questions. While knowledge increases by a mere factor of 322, the interface or potential of new discovery increases by a factor of 26,865!

Therefore, I again posit that greater understanding and knowledge is the fertile ground for more understanding, awe and knowledge, thus creating an ever increasing productive and wondrous cycle. So, the more we understand and know God through either scientific discovery or theology, the much more we will possess the capacity to know Him.

I also believe there is a corollary in human relationships. The more we trust and cooperate, eventually making ourselves vulnerable in mature relationships, the more the relationship will grow.

Lastly, as I describe in more detail in my book, God's Purpose in Creation, that divine purpose is no less than God willed to create a perfect companion, the redeemed of the Church and the body of Christ, to rule and reign with Him, as a part of Himself, forever over His special creation, the universe. When thus we 'know as we are known', the sphere of our knowledge of Him and the cosmos will equal His own, but paradoxically expand forever into infinity, as the universe itself continues to expand into the utter unknown still beyond itself.

Paul, in Romans 8, declares that the suffering of this present time is not worthy of being compared to the glory that will be revealed in us. What a wondrous thought, the seminal knowledge of which the poets of yesteryear began to see and record for us in a magical note.

Another way of thinking about this is the seeking and understanding of the fundamental and foundational truths in this life and in the cosmos, or perhaps what have we deemed to be a foundational truth that really is not? The dethroning of apparent and previously accepted foundational truth is usually cataclysmic and oftentimes results in a paradigm shift of cultural or individual thinking and operation.

In the cosmic-scientific realm, there was a belief that light in a vacuum always travels in a straight line and that time is strictly linear. Einstein theorized that both time and light and even space can be bent by gravity in his general theory of relativity. What holds true in usual circumstances becomes untrue in extreme circumstances.

Einstein then deduced that in the event horizon of a black hole, time would stop, and that light would be bent by gravity into it never to escape. Additionally, he deduced time would stop for an object traveling at the speed of light.

In science, truths are determined by rigorous empirical testing, and in 100 years of such tests, every one of Einstein's theories have survived.

In the religious-cultural realm in the second millennium AD, as man emerged from the yoke of Scholasticism in the Renaissance and the Enlightenment, erroneous ideas such as the earth being the center of the solar system and the idea of a flat earth were discarded. Ironically, neither of these changes threatened the idea of a Creator God or of His sovereignty. Today, it is perhaps time to do the same with the idea of a literal seven-day creation.

Science and religion have, for at least 2000 years, been entwined if not perceived to be in conflict, especially by dogmatic elements on each side. But if we examine carefully what we can hold as foundational truth, there perhaps emerges a beautiful picture of mutually confirming synergy in which we can see that as man learns more about the created universe, we then can better see and understand the Creator's purposes. Even the Apostle Paul clearly states this in Romans One of the Bible. Also, perhaps there are certain absolute and relativistic parallels through which we can discern and gain more insight into both.

What are the universal truths as we understand them? In the cosmic sense, mass (weight) and the linearity of time and space and the path of light are all relative to the place and perspective of the observer, while the speed of light in a vacuum is constant. This is a foundational truth in understanding the universe from a scientific perspective.

In the moral human rights realm, my son, David, once wrote an article on human rights using Thomas Jefferson as an example. He noted Jefferson wrote in the Declaration of Independence that all men are created (by God) as equals with inalienable rights, but yet he owned slaves and, in that day, male slaves were counted as 3/5 of a man on official records. He then posited that Jefferson was not immoral but simply, in his perspective, in this example, a man of his day. He further opined that if Jefferson were living in, say, 1870 after the Emancipation, he would not have owned slaves and would have perhaps abhorred the idea of doing so.

Women's rights have followed the same evolutionary course, and in our own time we face the same thorny issues of right to life at the both the beginning and end of life and gay rights as examples. He illustrated that the guiding foundational truth is indeed all men are created equal with the same rights. But even in a free society that was founded on this great truth, over time its application both by government and individuals changes based on the relative perspective of the day.

David was on target, not only in these thoughts but also in his own concluding declaration quoting Martin Luther King, 'The arc of the moral universe is long, but it bends toward justice!' He did not posit what type of gravitas or energy creates this arc but implies and I will now explicitly state, is the best efforts of moral men and women guided by the love, grace and mercy of the Creator.

We have discussed the foundational cosmic truth and moral-societal truth. Now, let's focus on the realm of religion. What is the foundational spiritual truth? It is, of course, the absolute truth that exists in the mind of God and is made known to us by His spoken and written word, the Bible, which tells us that God the Father created all things by speaking His Word, Jesus Christ, into the void of absolutely nothing. God declared to Moses, "My Name is I Am." That is, He exists in and of Himself and was not created. Jesus declared in John's Gospel, "I am the way and the truth and the life, and no one comes to the Father except by me."

Unfortunately, however, as Paul instructs in 1 Corinthians 13:12, with the Bible (in part oral) and (with the guidance of the Holy Spirit), we now only are able to understand the perfect will and truth of God imperfectly as in looking through a dark, wavy glass. He goes on to say that when we get to heaven, we will know as we are known. Only then will we perfectly understand God's perfect truth and will, which is the Living Word or Logos of God.

Just as surely as gravity bends physical light, both ill- and well-meaning men, and from their own erroneous perspectives, bend moral enlightenment and the spiritual light of God away from justice and toward the imprisonment of legalism.

May we also ask whether God, Creator of the cosmos and spiritual law, the latter of which He seemingly must uphold as the supremely just and ultimate judge of all things, of His own will and power bends the long arc of His truth out of mercy and grace and love toward justice in ways we do not understand? I believe this to be true, but it is certainly an inexplicable paradox. But the fact it is a paradox makes it no less true than the similar paradoxes of the three in one nature of the Trinity or the nature of Christ in being both fully divine and fully human.

In summary, there do indeed exist fundamental truths in realms of the cosmos and morality and the spiritual realm. These truths are neither contradictory nor mutually exclusive but are parallel and simultaneously beautifully interwoven. Understanding and applying all of them should help us understand the creation more thoroughly. Indeed, the complementary nature of these fundamental truths without question point to the One who created them all, the I Am God!

A special *PS* for the nerds who want to delve a little deeper is this missive on equating the curse with the thermodynamic concept of entropy.

Strong warning: Do not go here if you are not a scientific nerd!

The Creation and the Curse in the Light of Thermodynamics

"In the beginning, God created the heaven and the earth. And the earth was without form, and void; and darkness was upon the face of the deep. And the Spirit of God moved upon the face of the waters. And God said, 'Let there be light: and there was light.' … And God said, 'Let the waters under the heaven be gathered together unto one place, and let the dry land appear'; and it was so. And God called the dry land Earth; and the gathering together of waters he called Seas; and God saw that it was good. … And God said, 'Let there be lights in the firmament of the heaven to divide the day from night; and let them be for signs, and for seasons, and for days, and years' … And God said, 'Let the waters bring forth abundantly the moving creature that hath life.' … And God said, 'Let us make man in our own image, after our likeness and let him have dominion.'… So, God created man in his own image, in the image of God created he him; male and female created he them. And God blessed them, and God said unto them, 'Be fruitful and

multiply, and replenish the earth.' ...And God saw everything he had made, and behold, it was very good."

We know it well: The creation story from Genesis. From before the dawn of history, man has attempted to understand the meaning and the scope of creation, the creature in his finite mind trying to grasp the infinite being of the Creator God. Men have trodden the paths of ignorance, superstition, fear and scientific method in this attempt. Man would even attempt to make himself equal with God through his science, but in the end, man's science is nothing more than his latest, vain attempt, albeit best, to examine the footsteps of God.

The first law of thermodynamics states the concept of the conservation of energy and matter, that is within a closed system. Neither matter nor energy is created or destroyed, but only transformed from one state (of being) to another. The second law states that in these transformations, the dispersion of energy (and matter) within this system always becomes more random, disordered and less organized unless energy is applied to the system from another external system—the concept of entropy.

"In the beginning was the Word, and the Word was with God and the Word was God. The same was in the beginning with God. All things were made by him; and without him was not anything made that was made. In him was life; and the life was the light of men." John 1.

In the beginning, God spoke his all-powerful Word (the incarnation of which is Christ Jesus) into the void of the deep. This spiritual energy brought the universe into being. As God continued to speak over the next seven days, he successively brought into being the order and organization of the highly complex chemical, physical, biological and societal systems of the creation, including man. All was perfect, as God said, as he saw it was good.

And all would have remained perfect had it not been for the advent of sin. In Genesis chapter three, we learn of man's transgression against God and of man's punishment for his sin, the curse. The curse is, in essence, God's unleashing of entropy upon his creation of perfect systems, bringing disorder, disorganization, death and decay.

But praise be to God, in his infinite mercy and grace, He chose to speak again, bringing the incarnation of Jesus.

For God so loved the world, that he gave his only begotten son, that whosoever believeth in him should not perish, but have everlasting life. For God sent not his Son into the world to condemn the world, but that the world through him might be saved.

This Word of recreation through Christ's blood sacrifice and resurrection has reversed the spiritual and physical entropy of the curse. When lost, man accepts Christ as his Savior, the energy of the Word, recreates him spiritually and makes him a new creature. Romans chapter eight then tells us how the physical creation awaits Christ's second coming, at which time it will be freed from the curse. We, God's children, will then also be freed from the curse of physical death and decay, the effects of entropy, and given glorified bodies and live forever with God and Jesus in heaven, the new creation.

We then conclude that according to the very laws of nature, the universe could not have created itself or evolved spontaneously into a lower state of entropy (perfect order) but was indeed created into a state of perfection by the spoken Word of God, bringing its boundless energy into the face of the deep. And afterwards, when man brought the curse of entropy upon all the creation, including himself, God in his infinite mercy and grace once again spoke his all-powerful Word, negating entropy, and bringing in an everlasting perfect recreation.

How can we then, as God's children, not believe that He, who in the beginning created everything by speaking his Word into nothing and who has recreated us by the perfect sacrifice of his own Son, is not able to love, guide and protect us and our loved ones in the everyday trials of life and even death?

Of Medical School

Well, enough of the theology for now as we pivot back to education. I left the friendly confines of my home and my family and lifelong friends just after Christmas in 1973 for Memphis and Medical School.

It was my idea to arrive a few days early at the house of the Phi Rho Sigma Medical Fraternity. The weather was cold, dank and dreary, and perfectly befitting my newly discovered blue mood. I remember sitting there alone in my room and contemplating leaving for the comfort of home, but the desire to become a physician quickly trumped the coexistence loneliness. This internal battle continued throughout that first year as I transitioned from adolescence to manhood and as I learned medicine and to become a physician.

I, also for the first time, was surrounded by students who were as intelligent or more so than I, and believe me, there was a sense of competition. We were facing the specter of gross anatomy with cadaver dissection, embryology, pathology, histology—the anatomy of cells—biochemistry, physiology—the function of cells—and pharmacology that first year.

We were on a pass, fail or honors grading system, and I think I made honors in about a third of them. I could have made honors in biochemistry had I stayed and taken the elective honors exam, but I took the opportunity to go home after three months away.

About three miles from home, I was so excited I was stopped for speeding. One of my country friends, who was a well-known reckless driver, while witnessing my misguided misdemeanor, was having a private heehaw to himself. I severely chastised him when the trooper left; he just kept laughing!

I was glad my trusty dog, Skipper, still remembered me and was even more glad to taste my mamma's cooking and lie down in my own bed. She noticed I had lost 10 pounds and sent me back to Memphis with some of her high-octane food.

I gradually adjusted and befriended my new colleagues. At Phi Rho we played pool, volleyball and practical jokes. I don't know what came over me, but I pinned a classmate into his room, and he had to climb out his window that morning to get to class. If you don't know exactly what I did, look at a video on YouTube . I'll give you a clue: They had to take the door off its hinges to rectify the situation.

We also celebrated tall-tale-telling nights, and it seems one of our friends made a habit of telling such even when we were not supposed to be telling tall tales. He once told us he read in a news magazine the Saudi Arabians had bought 500,000 tanks from the Russians, at which one guy challenged there were not enough adults in Saudi Arabia to even drive that many tanks.

The same fellow, a wannabe artist, drew on our bulletin board a beautiful desert scene with a bunch of tanks as a prank. The tale teller had obviously seen the said scene and was hustling down the stairs screaming, "I'll kill him! I'll kill him!"

The artist at that point hid in the closet, but it turned out he was safe all along, as the other brother was upset about a situation at home.

I hate to admit it, but the tall tale telling and artistry both continued. One of our classmates was especially hyper and type A. One night, after dinner and before a gross anatomy test, he suddenly remembered he had forgotten to check a feature on his cadaver, and actually ran to the lab a mile away to satisfy himself. The artist drew a very neat picture of the runner with a large, hot, pulsating thyroid gland. Thereafter, JP had 'hyperthyroidism', like it or not.

Actually, his thyroid was fine. What had happened is that JP had become a 'gunner'—a delusion instilled in med school that physicians must be perfect. The pursuit of grades and the put downs of certain attending physician teachers at the simplest mistake made the pursuit of perfection inevitable. So sad.

I still vividly remember a neurology attending physician castigating one of us because the poor student did not perfectly perform the complicated process of a neurological exam on the first attempt in his career. After all, if he were able to do so, there would be no need for a teacher. The attending actually called the student an idiot. Basic training.

There was a short, ill-tempered, black headed, male surgery attending at the VA hospital whose favorite pass time was to pick on medical students; he was dis-affectionately known as 'Little Hitler'. One day, on rounds and in front of five fellow students and in front of a patient, I became his target. He asked me a series of simple questions for which I did not provide the specific answer he wanted to hear, although I did provide a few correct ones.

He told me I did not deserve to graduate from medical school, and to my credit, I remained silent. Then he accused me of being confused, to which I curtly replied, "Dr. P, I'm no more confused than anyone else around here when you start asking your damn fool questions to make students look like fools." The patient's eyes popped out, the other students melted, giggled and flowed under the bed, and Dr. P silently turned on his heels and left the room. I stood, somewhat proud and stoic. The incident was never mentioned.

But I became somewhat of a local hero and made honors in surgery.

As I write this after almost 50 years, I now see that this was when I most likely became infected with the other delusion taught in medical school—egotism.

There is a theory for this type of hazing. I think its misguided purpose was to instill a keen sense of confidence and independence, which are great assets in dealing with life and death situations, but if taken too far, it removes compassion and can lead to arrogance and disruptive behavior, which have been so prevalent in medicine.

Medical education was divided into two parts, the study of basic science and the learning of clinical medicine in a hierarchical system of attending, resident, intern, and student. And you guessed it, as oftentimes water is not the only thing which flows downhill. There is a much thicker, stinky substance which metaphorically does also.

Honestly, I was lost in my first clinical rotation, adult medicine, ironically my ultimate beloved specialty. My last rotation before graduation was surgery, and I hated the technical part and avoided it if possible. After all, had I aspired to be a mechanic, I would not have needed to go to medical school. I surely and sarcastically jest, of course.

The surgeons called the medicine doctors 'fleas' because we traveled in packs on rounds and scratched our heads while brainstorming together about all the possible diseases our patients might have. We always 'sucked' a lot of blood to perform tests in our diagnostic endeavors. Thus, 'fleas'. I am actually proud to be a flea.

In that last surgical rotation, I first came to enjoy and seriously learn to properly consider differential diagnoses for myself and to care for patients medically. I had become a competent graduate physician right on schedule and was ready to begin my Internal Medicine training at Methodist Central Hospital in Memphis.

PS: As usual, I forgot to tell you a key story. The night I decided definitely not to be a surgeon. It was in the middle of the night, and a young drug dealer had been shot in the thigh. The resident was concerned about the patient's femoral artery—main artery supplying the leg—being nicked, so off we went to surgery to explore the situation.

The surgeons, of course, were wearing cowboy boots and singing along with the country music on the radio. I remember the resident on the case was from Mossy Creek, TN. I was standing in the second row, half awake.

Then it happened!

The radio suddenly blared the worst song ever written and recorded, 'Drop Kick Me Jesus Through the Goalposts of Life'! All the true surgery types, including nurses, started hooting and hollering and singing along. It was an early form of surgical karaoke, I guess.

I just silently and reverently prayed to Jesus that if he would rescue me from this situation, I would never operate again. He did rescue me, and I never operated again. Thank you, Lord!

I am a real physician in Internal Medicine.

OF INTERNAL MEDICINE TRAINING AND OF BEING A PHYSICIAN

From 1974 through 1976, I attended medical school and received my MD degree in December 1976.

Education is only the beginning of the process of becoming a physician, as now I faced one year of training as an intern and two years as a resident under the tutelage of experienced doctors in the specialty. This occurred at Methodist Hospital in Memphis in monthly revolving rotations of the subspecialty disciplines such is medical oncology (cancer), cardiology (heart), pulmonology (lung) and so on.

Fortunately for me, I did a series of externships while in med school at Methodist starting IVs and assisting in surgery at night and on weekends and a medical school rotation of a month's duration with Dr. RB, a medical oncologist and the program chief for the training program. Therefore, when I started, I knew many people there already.

I began slowly but rapidly gained the skills in diagnosis, treatment and communication, which one must master in being a good physician. Every day we interacted with patients individually, on collective rounds with our fellow trainees both with and without the attending or overseeing doctor and learned to present our ideas and findings formally in both small and large groups.

The latter is best exemplified by the formal morning report that all trainees attended with the chief and at which all the new admissions from the previous day were subject to discussion, review and especially criticism.

My co-internal medicine resident was DM, who, like me, was raised on a farm, and we shared a similar country humor. One morning, a medical student gave a very good report on an admission, but at the end said something not so very astute. DM leaned over and whispered into my ear the most rural simile I've ever heard, "Mike, that's like a cow giving a whole gallon of milk and then peeing in it."

What could I say to that except grin in agreement?

There were also weekly specialty conferences at which attending physicians and trainees would present difficult cases both for the sake of learning and charting the best options for patient care.

I remember a funny incident at the cardiology conference where we were discussing porcine (pig) prosthetic (replacement) heart valves, which were new at the time. Someone asked how long we should expect a pig valve to last and be functional in a patient. A wise 'ole sage internist retorted from the back of the room, "How long does a pig live!" Chuckles. The answer to both is about ten years if the pig can avoid slaughter and donating his valves!

We certainly had our moments of good-hearted humor and playing practical jokes. There was an intern, BD, who loved to play jokes on his peers, and no one had been able to quite get even with him.

One month later, he and another intern were working under me as the resident on a private service. We were standing at the ward's nursing station when I spotted an older lady entering the women's restroom. She was a visitor, and I had no idea who she was.

"Hey, BD, the head nurse just went in there. Why don't you hold the door so she can't get out?", which he promptly proceeded to do. Meanwhile, the other intern and I stealthily slipped around the corner in order to observe. Suddenly, we hear from inside the privy, now a private prison, the scratching and pleadings of the would-be escapee while DB is holding the knob with all his might.

At about this time, he sees us laughing and realizes he has been had, so to speak, by one with a higher degree in practical joking than he. He lets go, and out walks this surprised and incredulous lady. For a brief moment, they exchange gazes and speechless thoughts, which are still unknown to me to this very day. I can only imagine! I wish I could say that this operation removed the desire from DB to play jokes, but alas, it did not. His illness was intractable.

I will always treasure my days at Methodist because it was there, under Dr. RB and other fine physicians, that I learned to think like, act like and become, I trust, a fine one myself. I learned to perform the duties and skills of my profession thoroughly and interact with both patients and staff to bring about the best outcomes. I came to believe the greatest skill that a doctor or any successful person in life can possess is the ability to gather, collate, and consider differential options of cause or diagnosis and, in turn, apply an appropriate plan or treatment: The skill of critical decision making.

I decided to offer this chapter for two reasons: First to give you some insight into medical training and how doctors think, and second to allow you to clearly understand that we are fully human with the same ideals, wants, needs and actions as you.

In 1980, I moved back home and applied my newly acquired abilities, thinking my education and training were over. But as we know now, while the formal parts were complete, the informal and practical were not yet at all completed and perhaps never will be.

Some mistakenly complain about the profession, but I would never choose any other. There is no way I could ever repay my patients, staff and the profession for all the blessings they have bestowed upon me.

Later in my career, I developed and attempted to live by my life statement of purpose. "I will use my God-given talents and abilities to enrich the lives of my family, friends, patients, friends and my community and beyond, and I will be blessed." I know of no profession other than medicine which would enable one to live out such a life mission, and it has indeed been a blessing.

PS: I will relate one last humorous occurrence, and I assure you I mean no disrespect to the patient in the story at all, as it is about self-inflicted humor on yours truly.

One day on rounds, as resident in charge, I had two interns and three visiting medical students. We were visiting an elderly lady who had kidney disease and was secondarily confused and disoriented.

I decided it would be a great opportunity to teach the students how to perform the orientation to time, place and person, part of a formal mental status exam. For Mrs. Smith in sequence, I asked her understanding of the current hour, day, date and year. She did not; I opined she was disoriented to time.

Medical students indicated their understanding.

Mrs. Smith, "Where are we currently?"

"Why, we are in heaven, of course."

I, to the students, "See, she is also disoriented to place." The students assented.

Next, I unwittingly pointed to her primary intern, whose last name just happened to be Moses. Do you see what is about to happen?

I to Mrs. Smith while pointing at Dr. Moses, "Do you know who this gentleman is?"

"No, I do not," she calmly replies.

I, in order to inform and clarify a matter of faculty and again unwittingly, "He is Dr. Moses, your doctor."

To which she perks up and shouts with the grandest enthusiasm, "Oh, yes! I just knew he would be here!"

Somehow, all of us professional doctors escaped professionally out into the hall, but you can only imagine the guffaw bestowed upon me.

Well, I deserved it, and I believe laughter is not only sometimes a good treatment for the patient but the physician also.

Perhaps even the best medicine means for a doctor to fulfill the old adage of: "Doctor, heal thyself."

Great advice, indeed.

I must speak of the AIDS epidemic, beginning in the mid-1980s and how it assisted my growth as a physician.

The epidemic was thrust upon us like a tsunami without warning and with cataclysmic change. The illness was a mystery; the diagnosis was one of certain death. In the beginning there was no direct treatment for it, but over the last 40 years, treatments have been developed which now achieve permanent remission, if not cure.

Since it emerged here in the gay community, there was also, sadly, a great social stigma associated with it. Some even called it God's judgment against the sin of homosexuality. In this context, let's just say in a non-judgmental manner that it was and is simply a viral illness transmitted via blood and other body fluids.

Many physicians avoided treating patients with AIDS, but many others saw it as a duty, perhaps even a blessing to serve. I attended many AIDS patients and acquired many in the gay community. I learned to respect them as fellow human beings, and gave my all in their treatment. In return, they appreciated and respected me.

This illness produced some of the greatest tragedies I witnessed as a physician. I cared for one man who presented in a coma and on a ventilator and who died 48 hours after presentation without our ever knowing his name. We simply knew him as John Doe.

I treated another very young man who presented with disseminated TB and heretofore unknown AIDS. I diagnosed both and began treatment for both, and he flourished. He went to visit family in NC and developed an acute fungal meningitis while there and died within days.

Perhaps most tragic were the young brothers who had hemophilia and who both died after contracting the virus from blood products. I was not their primary doctor, but was secondarily involved in their care. I, to this day, clearly remember the anguish of the parents.

Lastly, I had one very memorable gay, AIDS patient who survived for 4 years. I cared for him and his partner and several friends for many years. He was admitted to the hospital several times, and we became great friends. He taught me many things as we shared; and my horizons were expanded, and I trust my prejudices were diminished.

As can hopefully be seen, I became a better man and physician through this tragic time and experience. I learned not only how to give more of myself, but also how better to gracefully receive from others.

In the end, this is what the doctor patient relationship is all about in its deepest meaning. It is primarily for the benefit of the patient, but often times it can, out of shared vulnerability, respect and trust, produce mutual benefit and growth.

Our profession has definitely evolved and changed over the last few decades; and many believe and state that they would not become a physician again. I'll take the opposite view and will always believe that I made the right decision in becoming a physician, and have no misgivings at all, as the profession has been a great blessing to me.

Of Melynda

God blesses us, His children, in so many wonderful ways, but one of the best is through the gift of family and friends, perhaps most especially through godly spouses. After all, the love, sacrifice and growth in a godly marriage is a picture and a foretaste of our relationship with Christ. During the good times, we should enrich each other and during the bad times, we should assist each other to endure.

Few men have been blessed with two godly wives as I have. They have each blessed me in so many varied ways. And even though Melynda and Ruth were sisters, they were given very different personalities by their Father. Melynda, even though obviously human, was really never of this earth; she was born for heaven. She was ethereal and ephemeral. Her passing from this life, even though heartbreaking for me, was more of a translation than a death. On the other hand, Ruth, also a godly woman, is more practical and earthy.

Melynda and I were introduced on Jan. 20, 1975, at the beginning of my second year of med school, while she was enrolled in the BS nursing program. She, being a strong Christian, saw me at first as a ministry project, but after 2–3 months, I had fallen in love, and I decided I needed a wife rather than a minister.

Soon thereafter, on bringing her to the farm, I took her fishing and when our lines entangled with each other; I told her according to country lore that meant we were to be married. I bet it was the only time ever such a corny line of bait has been used as a proposal. Alas, the fish jumped off the hook that day.

By August, however, we planned our formal engagement to take place on a hill on the farm under the stars of a dark night. At about 11pm, as I presented the ring, we were heralded by a meteor shower. I won't say what happened next, and it is not because I don't remember!

We were married on Dec. 20, 1975, in my local Methodist country church, and began our life together. We thus rounded first base together and headed back to Memphis in Jan.

On a late afternoon in Dec. of 1978, Melynda, smiling, approached Dr. RB and the team at Methodist making rounds. She asked RB if she could have me for a few minutes, and when I returned, informed them of my impending fatherhood, RB said to me, "Michael, I think you best leave now and follow your wife home."

Great idea.

David was born the following August, and I was so excited that I yelled, "It's a boy!" before the obstetrician could. I told you, I like to preempt surgeons.

Melynda, being a BS trained RN, was my nurse and office manager when we established our solo Internal Medicine in Clarksville in 1980. All was right in the world.

Our second son, Jonathan, was born in 1982. Melynda started staying home to be a full-time mother, including being the only teacher in the 'Boys Home School'. She was great at it and taught David all the things that Reace had taught me.

When Melynda and I were married, we were in our early twenties and still maturing as Christians. However, she was ahead of me and taught me so many things about the deeper Christian life, including tithing. Melynda loved to give, and it was such a blessing for her. I never quite fully understood what so motivated her until one night, out of frustration, I accused her of giving for the wrong reason: Gaining affection she had not received as a child. I later asked forgiveness from her and God for this sin. I learned the deepness and richness of her true motive when she wrote the following note to me based on the story of the grateful woman in Luke:

"Mike, you said I am giving with the wrong purpose: Trying to gain affection. This is not so, but please read Luke 7:37-48. **I would deeply express verse 47, 'For she loved much.'** *He loved and loves me much. He has forgiven and still forgives much. That is why giving is so important to me. Whatever I give to the Lord is so very little compared to what he gave to me. But I love much, and giving makes me so happy."*

Melynda understood in her heart that giving to God in its purest and deepest and most loving form can never be formula driven or out of a sense of duty but only from a cheerful heart filled with love, appreciation and adoration for God and Christ and all that they have done for us first out of their unmerited love for us.

In her note, she also referenced 1 Corinthians, Chapter 9, in which Paul exhorts us to give cheerfully. She understood God wants to entrust His Kingdom's resources to those who will then cheerfully reinvest them in His work, becoming a veritable fountain of blessing for others. How many of us understand and practice this kind of motivation for giving today? Certainly, Simon the Pharisee did not, and I certainly did not until I saw it modeled and practiced by my wife. I must confess, I still do not to the same measure she did. But God so richly blessed me in so many ways by placing Melynda in my life.

Melynda passed from this life on April 22, 1987, which we will discuss later, but without her love, nurturing, and mentorship, I wonder if there would have been mission trips where I later gave of myself or especially the Bethany House, into which I know she would have enthusiastically immersed herself.

Melynda, I will always love you, as true love is not bound by time either in the past or future, but rather just is and always has been and always will be.

Amen.

When Melynda's cousin was married, she wrote to him a letter of advice, and when Jonathan and Randi married, I reworked it and added thoughts of my own I knew she would want to express for her son. When I read it at the rehearsal dinner, I can assure you there was not a dry eye in the house.

"Dearest Jonathan (and Randi),

I am so pleased about your wedding tomorrow; I want to wish you all the best for a very rewarding marriage and life together.

Beginning about six months before we were married, I was amazed at the number of people, both married and single, who were trying to advise me on how to be successfully married. I mean, there were people who were practically strangers getting into the act. So now, I guess you're thinking it is not my intention to do that—well, you're wrong!

After all, I have a big investment in you. God and I and your father gave you your life. Even though you don't recall with your mind, perhaps you do remember somewhere deeply within your heart my loving touch and my joy as I looked upon your face. I believe you somehow do remember those special moments and also how I cried with you night and day when you suffered with the colic for the first three months of your life. I guess that gives me the right to throw in my two cents now.

Marriage is probably the most demanding but also, at the same time, the most rewarding thing you will ever do in your life. You've got to give and give and keep on giving. That's because you are always also receiving. Randi will have to give to you at times when you don't even realize it, as will you for her.

One of the biggies in marriage is communication. You've got to make sure that you are really understanding what she is saying, not just what you perceive or think she is saying. So, until you have gotten into really open communication, it is probably best to say not only what you mean to say but also what you are not saying and what you don't mean to imply. It is good to say on occasion, 'Is there anything bugging you or is there anything you need to talk about?'

When you do have hard feelings for her or when you're mad, just confess it to the Lord and her, and ask for understanding and forgiveness. You never get anywhere in trying to cover over things. You've got to get them out in the open and work through them.

You must also realize that Randi's concept of what marriage should be will be influenced by her prior family life, just as your own concept will be. Then also realize it won't be purely either way exactly but a compromise between the two, which you will work out together over the time of your lives together. It will be unique to you and hopefully draw from the best of both of your preconceptions.

For example, we'd been married about three weeks when I was very sick with the flu with a fever of 103. Mike was planning to go to bowling practice with his team from the Phi Rho medical fraternity. Well, I had to learn it would take Mike a while to get used to having someone to look after. And he had to learn that the responsibilities of marriage don't just involve providing for the family and paying the bills, but also nurturing and caring for me, as I do for him.

But it is also true that you will need an occasional night out with the guys, even though she may hate to see you go. It is sort of a male inalienable right. Just make sure you always make plenty of time to be with Randi, other than eating and sleeping and watching TV. Play tennis with her and ride bicycles with her and travel with her and take long walks and talk with her.

Tell her I said it is also your inalienable right to watch TV football games and it might be good for her to watch along and get interested or to learn how to play bridge with you. Doing so has opened a whole new world for me as I even watch now while he isn't home sometimes. But be sure not to get impatient when she asks what is going on and why they are doing this *or that—just explain. Now comes the best part! You get to reciprocate and learn to enjoy and to participate in her interests and learn and grow together as a result.*

Also remember women are very sentimental. Never throw anything away unless you are sure it is something Randi is not saving.

Be sure to surprise her once in a while with a single rose or an inexpensive piece of jewelry—this will make life special. My uncle Lewis advised Mike to buy practical things, such as a hose or perfume, I needed and make them special by wrapping them. If you don't buy them, she will anyway, but if you buy them and make them a special surprise, she will brag about your being thoughtful and sweet.

When you deserve it, ask her to brag about you to you in caring for her and nurturing her and for being a good husband. Sometimes her praise will be the only praise you will hear, so cherish it and never take it for granted. And you do the same for Randi. Let her know on a regular basis how you appreciate her love and contributions. We all like to know we are appreciated and loved, and we, above all, cherish hearing it from our spouse.

Also, remember we women are cyclic; I know I had my emotional ups and downs. Just keep on loving and giving and giving and loving.

As for money, try to avoid debt and save for the rainy day that will surely come. Credit is a good thing if you remember to never charge more than you can pay in full each month as the bill arrives. Credit card interest will eat you alive. The one exception to this is borrowing to buy a home, which you need to live and grow in and hope the value will also grow over the years, unlike most things people buy on credit which loses value. So, just go slow on acquiring things and avoid trying to keep up with your friends in doing the same.

I got depressed when I saw so many of my friends having babies as I did want to be a mother and for us to have a family. So many of the girls at the hospital had kids already, but we just couldn't afford one right then. But we waited for God's time and our time. For then, it is just so neat getting to really know the person I married.

Get involved with Randi's family and do things with them. I helped Mark with preparing his tobacco field and raising his garden. Find out how you can help or do fun things with her family. And don't be afraid to accept help from them as when Mike's family gave us some furniture to get started with. Gracefully accept such offers and appreciate and take good care of such gifts. Learn to both give and receive within your new family, as that is what family is for.

Now that I've stuck my nose in where it doesn't belong, I'll finish up. By the way, after I finish this piece of advice, I feel confident that I can keep from ever interfering again. But I feel even more confident that Ruth will skillfully and lovingly continue to care for you in my place, as she has these last 26 years. However, I hope you will never forget me or ever cease loving me.

And I do want you to see you forever happily married. You can do it. It is workable if you remember to turn to the Lord for strength and to help and always love one another as He has loved us.

Finally, at times, ask the Lord to tell Randi how much you love her on your behalf. He knows how to do it better than you can. Once, Mike was on call at the hospital and I could not reach him. So, I just asked the Lord to tell him how I loved him. Early the next morning, he called me and told me he had awakened with an overwhelming feeling of love for me and how he could not sleep without first calling and telling me about it. Fantastic! Tell Randi how you love her at least seven times per day.

Above all, I want so much for you to be happy together and to love God.

Love always,

Your mother in Heaven,

Melynda"

After I read this, Ruth, then from her heart, spoke of her own love for her sister and how she had given her life in love and devotion for David and Jonathan.

At this point, the house was floating away on a tide of love and tears.

PS:

Melynda's Song

You came into my life,

One soft summer's day.

Brought there by God,

And in Heaven's sway.

Love was so tender,

In the innocence of our youth,

As we shared life together,

That's the honest truth.

I was never afraid,

And lived without fear,

Because I lived each day,

Knowing your heart was always near.

Living with you,

I was as happy as a wife could be,

Living and growing,

And just being me.

Over the years,

As you gave me your love;

While content in your care,

I always thanked the Lord above.

Our time together,

Was all too brief.

But my life with you,

Was oh, so sweet!

But as the seasons are carried

On the wings of time,

So must our lives here end,

When the clock bell chimes.

God drew my soul to heaven,

On the gentle breeze of His voice,

As the leaves of autumn float on the wind,

To a place of its choice.

So do not lament for me,

And always remember and never forget;

We shall meet again one day in heaven,

Forever together, with our Father and Lord!

Thoughts from 1987
Mike Carrigan

Of Tragedy and Suffering Part 1

April 22, 1987, dawned as a perfect day for me. I was blessed by the grace of God with a wonderful wife of eleven years, Melynda, and two delightful children, David, 7, and Jonathan, 4. My medical practice, which I loved, was thriving with wonderful patients and a great staff. I was also blessed with a wonderful extended family and a great network of friends.

So, when the sun rose on that beautiful spring morning, all was right with the world. As I kissed Melynda goodbye for the day, I was really kissing her for the last time; it was our last moment together on earth. In a matter of hours, my world was about to change forever.

Unknowing what my future held, I continued with my perfect day by proceeding to the hospital to make my morning rounds. Melynda would soon leave the house to drive the kids to school. About 8am, I received the phone call no one ever wants to receive. "Dr. Carrigan," a voice said, "your family has been involved in a severe wreck on the bypass and your wife is critical, as is one son, but the other son is okay." Stunned and horrified, I rushed to the ER.

Melynda was rolled in on a gurney and I mustered the courage to approach her, as there was no other doctor there.

What would I see?

What would I feel?

I could see that she was in shock from blood loss, and obviously dying. I had already prayed God's will be done for her, and I knew she was in His hands. The surgeon soon arrived, and, with my permission, she was whisked away for emergent, desperate surgery.

I was trapped in an overwhelming whirlwind of events beyond my control, but I knew my God was there with me!

David also arrived on a gurney, and although he was pale, he appeared stable. He only had a broken arm and a severe concussion but would be watched in the neuro-trauma unit for two days, ultimately making a full recovery, we thought.

In retrospect, I now see how many ways his life was changed.

As was originally reported to me, Jonathan was fine. He arrived at the ER in the arms of a friendly policeman who had been sent by God to minister to him. I later learned over the years that there were several other kind people who attended to my family that morning.

After Melynda was taken into surgery, I was alone for only a few minutes before several of my nursing friends took me into their proverbial arms and showered their love upon me.

I soon began making calls to family and friends. When they arrived, we prayed and waited, fearing the worst while hoping for the best. In my clinical mind, I knew what the outcome would be, but I was hoping to be wrong. After almost two hours of surgery, the surgeon explained he had done all he could. Melynda's internal injuries were too severe, and she had lost too much blood to survive.

My beloved wife had died.

WHY?

What had happened to cause such a thing? I was told she had pulled out of a side road into the path of a truck, but I would never know the answer as to why she did that. What I struggled most to understand was why my loving heavenly Father, whom Melynda had served with such fervor all of her short life, would allow such a thing to happen.

Shortly thereafter, as I gazed down at her body, I had an indescribable peace knowing she was in the presence of God in heaven and that this was God's plan for her. He surely also must have a plan for me and my children. And, indeed, He did.

The next day, my new faith and peace would be sorely tested, as I would have to tell David of his mother's death and what that meant for her and him. God was with us in that moment, the most difficult time in my entire life.

I spoke at Melynda's funeral of her faith and abiding love and what she had given and taught me in life.

The only thing I could not face was the shoveling of dirt on her grave at the Davidson Graveyard.

God and I together in that forlorn, lonely moment walked over to the graves of my ancestors. In my heart I heard, "Do not fear, for I am with you, and Melynda is also here with me and glorified. I will be with you in this journey."

Ruth will take up the story in the next chapter.

This, of course, is an example of tragedy in my life. We all experience similar tragedies, as no one is immune. Not only do we suffer accidental death, divorce, financial ruin and devastating sickness, things largely beyond our control, we also suffer the worst evil Satan can mete out, and that mankind can perpetrate on his fellow man: Murder, rape, infanticide, genocide and all the rest, including the crusades and the inquisitions that were the works of God's own Church.

Indeed, why does a loving God allow such tragedy to occur? What is his ultimate purpose in this? Even though He does not prevent it, how, and more to the point, will He comfort us amid it?

This was the first in a long train of tragedies in my life, but more on these later, and the why.

PS:

Life Changes

Grains of sand,

Time after time,

Flowing in and out with the tides.

Ever changing, never resting,

From eternity past,

Into eternity future.

Leaves and trees,

Year after year,

Growing and maturing with the seasons.

Ever changing, never resting,

From eternity past,

Into eternity future.

Raindrops and snowflakes,

Season after season,

No two ever alike.

Ever changing, never resting,

From eternity past,

Into eternity future.

Men and women,

Life after life,

Growing and learning with the tides.

Ever changing, never resting,

From eternity past,

Into eternity future.

The hand of God,

Eon after eon,

Directing time and tide.

Never changing, never resting,

From eternity past,

Into eternity future.

Grief's Journey

Who is grief,

But that Dark Villain,

Who gallops into the innocent soul,

Taking the wellspring,

Of its refreshing water,

And devouring the fodder,

Which sustains its heart?

The pangs of grief today,

Not only steal,

The joys of tomorrow,

But also rush somehow,

Even into yesterday,

Covering forever its view,

With a pallid sorrow.

Grief does not gentle,
Just rest within us,
But etches its wrinkle,
Upon our brow,
And becoming inherent,
As an eternal brother,
Inside and within our being.

Not an enemy,
To be expunged or defeated,
But by our will,
And the power of God,
To be tamed, subdued.
A worthy new partner,
In the trials and joys,
Of life's tomorrows.

Christ, Himself bore,
Our grief, sin and sorrow,
Wearing them as a cloak,
And upon His head,
As thorny, painful crown.
So as to us,
All love and grace do abound!

Thus, In today's,

Darkest hours,

God's Angel of Peace,

Though we do not see nor sense her,

Sent there our hearts to stir,

With love and grace.

Ne'er again,

To be the same,

As we are forged by holy fire,

More like Christ,

'Ere to be.

Heartbroken to love and to inspire,

With eternal empathy,

Friends in their blackest hour.

Grief thus leads,

On a godly journey,

Becoming more like Christ,

As agent of His love here,

And forever in eternity,

His love and grace,

Fore'er to share!

OF RUTH

Hello, my name is Ruth Collins Carrigan, and it is April 21, 1987.

I was raised in Nashville, Tennessee, one of the middle two of four daughters.

We were a middle class and pedestrian family. My mother was a wonderful person who struggled to raise her daughters correctly and uprightly in the face of a husband, my father, who was incapable of loving any of us.

There was an absence of physical abuse, but the constant emotional turmoil hung over our house and lives like a plume of dark dust and hot vapor over an erupting volcano, stifling our spirits.

It was no help that we attended a very legalistic church in which we, as adolescent girls, were forbidden to wear shorts or makeup or go to the swimming pool or movies or play cards.

The church, also in my presence, voted one night to deny me membership because of a political division in order to prevent my voting on it. But I did not understand; I was just wounded.

My father neglected the house, and it was condemned when a piece of plaster fell off the ceiling, landing on me in my bed. My mother finally took us to a better apartment and away from my father.

Can you imagine all the emotional problems this caused?

I found a job at a printing company and plotted my escape in work and marriage. I eventually learned to be an excellent EKG technician and worked in a west Nashville hospital where I met several country music stars and prominent people, including Dr. PK, cardiologist, who was a great encouragement to me.

I, however, made a huge mistake in marriage, and divorced after four years. By this time, Melynda and Mike had established their medical practice in Clarksville, and they invited me to join them, performing simple nursing duties and EKGs.

I remember surprising Mike by diagnosing an acute heart attack on an EKG once. My confidence grew, and I followed Melynda's lead and pursued a degree in nursing.

This was greatly emotionally facilitated by my mother moving in with Mike and Melynda and children. Mike worked a lot at night; thus, I spent a lot of time there with them and the kids.

I was doing well in school and enjoying life when my mother developed a very aggressive cancer, diagnosed in Jan. 1984. She then died on my 34th birthday on August 1st. Again, life had dealt a devastating blow. I had to manage all this, school and work part-time, but I persevered and graduated with a BS degree in nursing in front of my proud Clarksville family in May 1986.

I am very proud of the fact I promptly began working in the intensive care unit of the bone marrow service at Vanderbilt. There, I quickly matured as a nurse in taking care of the sickest of the sick.

Years of adverse circumstances and tragedies conquered, I was considering missionary work, maybe in India, with Mother Teresa. Thus, on the night of April 21, 1987, I am going to bed as content and optimistic as I have ever been in my entire life.

The next beautiful day dawns uneventfully. The phone rings. It is Mike speaking softly, "Melynda and the boys have been involved in an accident on the bypass. Melynda is in surgery and not expected to live.

David has a severe concussion and Jonathan is okay. Please come," he urgently said.

"Of course."

I was numb and on arrival at the hospital, I don't even remember the drive.

The nurses took me to Mike and other family members.

"Melynda is still in surgery; we are just waiting and praying."

The room was full of palpable anxiety and kinetic energy, dread and expectation.

Then the news came finally from the Dr., "We did all we could, but ..."

That's all I hear, followed by shock and denial. Wails of tears ensue by all except Mike. He is a calm, stoic rock.

We, Mike, Mark, his brother and I, are ushered to an anteroom in surgery to visit my sister. I am fearful; Mike is still calm. There are no external injuries, but her face is void and body limp and lifeless. My sister is gone, dead; passed is too innocent, dead is the right word. Dead!

Horror.

We all hugged and kissed her; tears flowed.

Mike, firmly: "Melynda has blessed us and loved us, and we and God will get through this."

We then returned to the ER and David and confer with his neurologist. He is concerned about his head injury and recommends transfer for observation to a Nashville hospital with a neurotrauma unit. I accompanied him. The night is a long, hellish and sleepless night, but David is doing well and will be okay.

I did not know it then, but I became David's mother that night.

It is now the next morning and Mike and his best friend, JJ, have arrived to visit and tell David about his mother. My aunt and first cousin are here as well.

Mike, "David, I love you; how's it going?"

David uttered a soft, "Okay."

"David, you know you were in a terrible accident yesterday?"

"Yes."

Mike finally begins to tear up. "David, your mother did not make it; she died in the accident. She is now in heaven with God."

Tears gush again. What a moment!

It is now two days later at the funeral. This is the easy part, I think. What will happen later? My cardiology friend and his partner arrive; Mike also knows them as friends and professionals now.

Mike has selected grand music from the 'Messiah'. Now, he rises to speak of his wife, my sister. There is an overflowing crowd of several hundred present.

Mike tells of his love for Melynda and ends by saying, "One day, I will see you in heaven." He taps the casket. The deafening silence is broken only by sobs.

The cemetery certainly provides neither peace nor solace. The preachers preach, but the words are silent for me as they fly away like birds on a spring day. I am dwelling in my bubble, semi-protected.

On the way back to the house, Mike seems a little nervous.

"Ruth, I hate to ask you this, but would you consider giving up your job to stay with us and care for the boys for a few months?"

Quickly, I say, "Yes, duty calls, anything for my sister and her children."

The details are worked out but are not important. I have become a temporary mother.

Two nights later, David is readmitted to the hospital with bruised intestines from a seat belt injury. It is little more than a temporary setback.

David did not return to the first grade, as he excelled. Earlier in the year, he had been taken to the third grade by his teacher to explain foreign currency exchange and the nature of eclipses.

David, crying, to the two teachers visiting him at home, "Will I fail the first grade if I don't return?"

"Don't worry, David, don't worry."

God bless them.

So, I cared for the children, took them to school and loved them.

Visiting the pediatrician, our friend, he, after a few months, asked me out of love and concern, "Are you going to be permanent?"

That was a question pregnant with multiple meanings, as it turned out. Many of our friends were thinking the same.

Mike became nervous again and one night, of all things, slipped a note under my door expressing his great admiration for me ... and burgeoning love!

He is sort of bashful when it comes to matters of the heart, so I must kiss him first. We become secretly engaged in August and are married on St. Thomas in the Virgin Islands the next June. Our friends are very happy; some were not. One opined our love is like a rose growing from a rock.

Our life together is normal, I guess, with all the good and bad, but full of unusual tragedies which we have survived together.

I love my family and my home.

Ruth Carrigan

PS:

My writing on Ruth:

"He that findeth his life shall lose it: and he that loseth his life for my sake shall find it." Matthew 10:39.

When Melynda died, I was devastated, but I believed God had a plan for me and my two young boys. I had a very busy medical practice and faced raising my sons alone. I don't really know if I acted as I often have in a medical crisis which usually demands resolute and quick action or out of faith or out of sheer panic and desperation, but I asked Ruth to join me for a period to help with the boys.

Only one year before, she had completed her BS degree in nursing at 36 and she had been divorced for ten years. She had steadfastly worked so hard for her degree, and she was working at Vanderbilt Hospital's bone marrow transplant unit. Certainly not out of any sense of secondary gain for herself and not even primarily from a sense of duty, but rather, I believe, from the same deep understanding of giving which had motivated Melynda, Ruth freely decided to give up the life for which she had struggled and to invest it in the lives of her sister's children.

I can't explain it, but as time went on, God instilled in us a sense of deepening respect and admiration and, finally, love for each other. We were married on June 13, 1988. Ruth has been such a blessing for me over the last 34 years, and I know I have for her, also. We have laughed together; we have cried together, and we have lived life together. And we have served God together at home and on many foreign medical mission trips. As one of our friends said, "Only God can grow a rose from a rock."

I humbly offer the above examples of how our Father so mightily loves and blesses us. We should all now use this knowledge as we demonstrate our love for Him in the daily act of cheerfully giving our lives in service for Him in blessing others and in taking the Gospel to the lost. As we have discussed, this will facilitate our own sanctification is this life, thus preparing us for our eternal relationship with God.

PS:

Tribute for Ruth

Your cheeks are like roses,

Your eyes mirror bright,

Your soul a signet,

Your spirit a light,

Which shines into the cold steel night.

You brighten my day,

You color my way,

You have made my heart soar,

Into clouds of joy,

From the depths of despair,

Because you were there.

Be kind to me and comfort me,

As I will for thee.

This one prayer I pray,

That our love will never fade away,

But will last forever and a day!

I also offer this poem written for Randi and Jonathan in celebration of their union in marriage and remembering the love in my own marriages:

The Union of Love

The Father's love,

Transcending heaven,

As the promise of a rainbow,

And piercing man's heart,

With the explosion of thunder!

The Son's love,

Begun in all humility,

Of lowly human birth,

And perfected in anguish of blood sweat,

And in the agony of the cross!

The Father's love,

Shone into our hearts,

As golden sun drops,

And flooding our souls,

With healing crimson blood.

Grandparents' love,

Freely given to their cherubim like child,

In a loving embrace,

A watchful eye,

And in wonderful expectation.

A mother's love,

Expressed as a life given,

After the pattern of Christ,

And in an adoring smile,

And shared in a simple embrace of hands.

Another mother's love,

Spontaneously expressed,

And of a life freely given,

And flowing from her heart,

As soothing water from a boiling spring.

A lost mother's love,

Her words of wisdom,

Blowing like a soft wind across the years,

Into our souls,

And plucking the strings of our hearts.

The love of the fathers,

One in giving his beloved away,

After the pattern of our Father,

And the other immersed,

In the wonder and beauty of it all.

A groom's love,

Expectantly waiting,

As he sees the approach of his beloved,

Much as is Christ as He waits,

For His Father's call, in heaven.

The bride's love,

Unbridled in a glowing countenance,

Which would melt all the snows on the earth,

And which is a foreshadow of our looking into the soul of God,

And finally, and fully knowing His love for us.

The love of families,

Newly joined,

And praying for their beloved children,

As they in union send them from the nests,

Into the peril and adventure of life.

The love of friends,

Joining in celebration,

Remembering special moments of the past,

And sharing in the anticipation,

Of the excitement and promise of the future.

A very special day,

As our hearts were joined,

In a very special way,

By our Father God forever,

In the Union of love!

Mike Carrigan

10-09-13

On the marriage of Randi and Jonathan on 10-05-13

Of Tragedy and Suffering Part 2

Thank you for reading along with me thus far. Let's further consider the concept of suffering. Losing Melynda, to be sure, was the most traumatic event in my life. She had an uncanny intuition. She had also certainly tasted far more trials and tribulations than me in our respective lives.

No more than a month before she was killed, we were discussing the same thing one morning. In a very loving way, she very gently advised, perhaps even warned me, one day God would allow the rosy-colored glasses of life to be removed from my eyes.

Prophetic?

Perhaps. Less than a month later, she was gone.

And very much to be sure, the glasses had been at least damaged.

After her death, it took a while for tragedy to strike again, but strike again it did.

And again.

And again.

And again!

One super 'religious friend' actually opined that my family had a generational curse of the Old Testament variety as the cause of the calamities, which I quickly dismissed as a wicked superstition.

You see, in our culture, so many people build a web of comfort in setting a false belief that God protects us from any harm in this life. It just is not so! In fact, Christ in the Upper Room on the eve of His own crucifixion promised the disciples suffering and persecution in this life. This contradicts the modern American gospel of comfort, certainly the absence of suffering, if not the belief of outright prosperity.

David, our older son, suffered from severe depression and Asperger's Syndrome, from which he was forced to leave medical school and give up on his dream of becoming a doctor.

He was studying actuarial science and had passed the first two exams on his own. In June 2014, he was visiting home from Memphis after attending a conference in Atlanta when he suddenly developed chest pain and was misdiagnosed with indigestion by a local physician. Two days later, he suddenly passed away in our house at 34.

I found him sitting on the floor in the basement, where he slept in my man cave. I cried holding him; Ruth was devastated. She stills speaks of seeing her son being zipped in a black bag and carted out of the house.

I and others still remember seeing Jonathan solitarily and silently standing over his brother's lifeless body at the funeral home, as one friend said, a holy human moment.

Ruth was led to have a friend sing 'All Is Well with My Soul' at his service. Sometime later, we found in his journal the words of his Christian journey and faith of salvation recorded.

Handwritten on one of the inside covers were these words:

"When peace like a river attendeth my way

When sorrows like sea billows roll

Whatever my lot, Thou hast taught me to say

It is well, it is well with my soul

It is well (it is well)

With my soul (with my soul)
It is well, it is well with my soul.

Though Satan should buffet, though trials should come
Let this blest assurance control
That Christ (yes, He has) has regarded my helpless estate
And has shed His own blood for my soul
It is well (it is well)
With my soul (with my soul)
It is well, it is well with my soul.

My sin, oh the bliss of this glorious thought (a thought)
My sin, not in part, but the whole (every bit, every bit, all of it)
Is nailed to the cross, and I bear it no more (yes!)
Praise the Lord, praise the Lord, O my soul!
It is well (it is well)
With my soul (with my soul)
It is well, it is well with my soul
Sing it as well
It is well (it is well)
With my soul (with my soul)
It is well, it is well with my soul.

And Lord, haste the day when my faith shall be sight
The clouds be rolled back as a scroll
The trump shall resound, and the Lord shall descend

Even so, it is well with my soul!

It is well (it is well)

With my soul (with my soul)

It is well, it is well with my soul

Sing up to Jesus, it is well!

It is well (it is well)

With my soul (with my soul)

It is well, it is well with my soul."

And so it is, both with the living and physically dead in Christ.

In July 2016, I received another one of those calls of which no one wants to be a part. CS, Randi's mother, called to tell me Jonathan, 34, leaving for work, had an accident and has been taken to Vanderbilt. She and her husband were frantically on the way to Tennessee.

Indeed, his SUV would not start and as he was pushing it out of the garage, it got away from him, and rolled along with him down a 10-foot embankment into his neighbor's backyard, finally crashing into a tree.

In Jonathan's own words:

"I am stunned and in pain and try to stand but cannot. I barely muster enough strength to call for help one or two times. Suddenly, men appear and call for help."

It was rather miraculous as the men had been working on a roof across the street from his house and somehow heard the clamor and call. He sustained several broken ribs, a crushed pelvis and ankle and a torn pelvic artery requiring 24 units of transfused blood. This is about 2.5 times the blood volume of an adult male.

When I arrived, I saw my son on a ventilator, sedated and with the obligatory myriad of tubes. Randi was devotedly by his side.

He spent two months in the hospital and rehab and happily came home to his wife and 4-month-old son, Daniel. He had missed half of his son's life, but they could now watch TV together from the hospital bed.

Two days later, another frantic call from Jonathan. Daniel was found not breathing and taken to the hospital; it looked bad. Before I could leave the house, as Ruth had left for Franklin an hour away, the local deputy visited me at home. The news was the worst—death.

This time, I was the one to call Randi's mother.

Ruth went home to be with our son, and I went to the hospital.

I held the lifeless body of my only grandson.

Unbelievable, but undeniable and real. Death has stolen again.

I tried to console my daughter, but she did not even know I was holding her, lost in a mother's whirling world of the worst kind of grief.

We then had a graveside service on a beautiful late summer afternoon in north Georgia. Beauty surrounded us; we were serrated by the reality of the loss of our precious Daniel.

Randi had sung 'Oh Danny Boy' for him in love and we now heard it beautifully sung for us as a solo, with its notes rolling through the Georgian hills and meadows, finally filling the sky with sadness and hope.

"Oh, Danny boy, the pipes, the pipes are calling
From glen to glen, and down the mountain side
The summer's gone, and all the rose is dying
'Tis you, 'tis you must go and I must bide.
But come ye back when summers in the valley
Or when the valley's hushed and white with snow
'Tis I'll be here in sunshine or in shadow

Oh Danny boy, oh Danny boy, I love you so.

But if you come, and all the flowers are dying

And I am dead, as dead I well may be

He'll come and find the place where I am lying

And kneel and say an "Ave" there for me.

And I shall feel your soft thread above me

And In my grave where riches sweeter be

For you will bend and tell me that you love me

And I'll shall rest in peace until you come to me.

And I'll shall rest in peace until you come to me."

The caretakers then took the little white box and placed it in the ground. My own son released the pain of his grief in a wail of pain, and I was powerless to help except to briefly hold him in love.

All the rest left the gravesite except for SS and me and I motioned for him to assist me as our shovels commit the body of our dear grandson to the earth.

Daniel is not there; he is with Jesus.

So, these then are my final thoughts on suffering, tragedy, tribulation and evil in this life and why God allows it.

And I think I, by now, have experienced enough in my personal walk and assisting patients with the same to offer an opinion and advice.

Yes, I am fully aware of the OT story of Job and the NT narrative of James 1 of the virtues of suffering. But stop to consider the greatest narratives on the subject in the NT: Romans 8 and the Upper Room Discourse in John 14-17. They are very consistent, as they both clearly state suffering and tragedy will come as we are indeed joint heirs of it with Christ along with His glory. Christ explicitly states that persecution (and suffering) is in and of the (fallen) world while not mentioning God as their source. Both state that God will provide comfort and wisdom from the Holy Spirit and that we have Christ as our intercessor High Priest and that none of it, even death, can separate us from the Father's love or the glory (by being perfectly one with Him and thus of Him in partaking of His divine nature as the body and Bride of Christ), He has for us in eternity.

Lastly, Paul states all things will work for good for those who are called to His purpose. God primarily 'allows' pain and suffering in this life under the curse so that lost souls will ask (free will and free agency) His son for salvation, building the body of Christ (the future most glorious temple of Haggai). This is His general permissive will for the church age.

Both Christ and Paul use the metaphor of childbirth not only to capture the pain but also the expectancy of joy and glory. I would add the metaphor that this fallen world and all its evil and suffering, which were precipitated by man's sin, becomes the fiery cauldron of our salvation. Thus, nowhere do I see in these important passages any hint that God proactively causes or 'allows' concurrently pain, evil, persecution or suffering, much the less for an important life lesson.

The plague that killed more than half the population of Europe was an infectious disease, not an evil spirit or God sent. The Inquisitions and Crusades were planned and enacted by evil men. All wars have been planned in the evil hearts of men, including the Holocaust of Hitler and purges of Stalin, in which 50 million souls were killed.

The persecutions and martyrdoms of the saints over the ages saddened God and were of evil men, not our God. Consider abortion. People naturally suffer and die of natural diseases.

I wonder what spiritual lesson could possibly be learned by a victim of Alzheimer's disease when the patient is in a vegetative state, wasting away?

My wife died because she pulled out in front of a plumbing truck, not because God willed it, physical law.

My son died of a heart infection because he saw an incompetent Dr.

My other son almost died because he tried to stop a truck from rolling down a hill.

My first grandson died because he simply stopped breathing (SIDS)

The tenets of Calvinism, including the belief that God ordains and/or permits all events in every day of our lives and so prevalent in the church today, is a major factor in these erroneous teachings. It provides such a comforting system in explaining the good that comes into most lives but falls totally apart in explaining the differential evils and suffering, which rain into the lives of most.

The concept neither is consistent with the impartial and loving God of scripture nor the realities of life of which I have endured and witnessed others endure. In the end, these teachings do not bring comfort but just more suffering and guilt.

In closing, I offer the following poem of the specter of death and of the life and hope we have in God.

The Face of Death

Oh Death!

I knew thee not in my mother's womb

As there by her love

I was consumed.

Bursting forth

Into wondrous life,

I had no idea

Of your strident strife.

But er'e there you were
With cold eye on me
As in my mind
Life lasts through for all eternity.

Then one day
On wicked black wing,
You stole my wife
As I first felt your ven'mous, sordid sting!

In her pale face
Peace I did see,
While in my achy heart
Welled up a mighty hate for thee!

On a similar day
At me, you stared
As your languid look
Made me sorely scared.

Into my heart
Raced your pangs of fear
But with my mind I clung
To my Savior dear.

I lived to see
Another day
But to you, a debt I owe
Which I must pay.

One by one
You have taken friend
Then my son you stole
On stolid wind.

As I looked into his
Cold, blue, lifeless face,
I knew, my son
I could never replace.

As a fiendish foe
As you have been to me,
But to some a friend
You seem to be.

Born of Satan
You roam the earth
To make mankind sing
Of dirge and dearth.

But a day will come

When your reign will end

As face to face with Christ, you will be.

New age of life will then begin,

Which will last through all eternity!

The Pursuit of the Infinite Life, Sanctification and Glorification

We have reviewed life, faith, suffering and salvation. The question is: What does all of this mean for us as Christians today in living our lives and in looking forward to eternity?

Philippians chapter 2 tells of Christ leaving His glory in heaven in obedience to the Father and in all humility and sacrifice to serve us. Paul instructs in the same chapter, we are to follow this example in the working out (not for) our salvation.

Paul further instructs in Romans 12, we are to sacrifice our lives in service, which becomes a special and pleasing automatic to Him in heaven.

Jesus said one must give up his life to find it.

This is, in my opinion, what the infinite life means in this life, becoming more like our Lord daily.

In John chapter 3, Jesus instructs Nicodemus, *"Are you the teacher of Israel, and do not know these things? Most assuredly, I say to you, we speak what we know and testify what we have seen, and you do not receive our witness. If I have told you earthly things and you do not believe, how will you believe if I tell you heavenly things? No one has ascended to heaven but He who came down from heaven, that is, the Son of Man who is in heaven."*

Paul in 2 Cor. 12 Paul describes his glimpse into glory and relates what he has seen as inexpressible; and earlier in the same letter, *"Eye hath not seen, nor ear heard, neither have entered into the heart of man, the things which God hath prepared for them that love him.* " A glimpse into the infinity of glory.

In 2006, as I previously described, I had a similar intimate encounter with God, as did Isaiah in the temple. On the razor thin edge that exists between life and death, I looked at the specter of my death and found the perfect, infinite reality of my God:

"I then remember how I could see in my mind's eye my Lord sitting at the right hand of God interceding for me and how He was there with me in the car as my Good Shepherd leading me beside the still waters and bringing me perfect peace. I realized whether I lived or died, I was in His hand and nothing else mattered. I believed, then and now, that when my time to die does come, I will have that same real peace. In that moment, I realized my relationship with my God was perfect. All my abilities and talents, my family, my friends, my church and yes, even my earthly toils and interpersonal strife and sins were all totally meaningless. Me and my life, the good and bad, became nothing in that wonderful moment, and He became perfectly everything. He already was and is; I had just not really known it until then."

I guess that was the Isaiah moment of my life. Part of me wants to stay there, in that moment, in the temple with God, and in His time, in heaven, that will be the case forever. But for now, God is calling me, us, to heal our relationships with each other and to lead our churches, our families and our businesses in doing the same. Only then will we become His salt and life for our communities and the world, and nothing else will then seem to matter anymore.

I was touched by the mighty hand of God in this transcending moment of infinity.

As the Lord inferred, heaven is definitely a reality beyond what we can understand or articulate in this life. God is perfectly sovereign, and He will bring His purposes to complete and final fruition in the physical and spiritual universe and beyond time in eternity past and into eternity future, infinity. His will is the matter and flux of all reality. However, in His wisdom and within His permissive purposes in accomplishing His ultimate will of the birth of redeemed man as His perfect companion, He has created within this totality of His sovereign will a special bubble of sorts.

This bubble is a mere ripple in true reality, which we call finite time and space and which began at creation and will end when God sends His Son to redeem His church out of them and beyond them to exist in eternity beyond time and in heaven with Him where He existed alone in eternity past. In this bubble He, as noted above, allows the free wills of lost men and Satan to coexist along with natural and spiritual laws, bringing suffering and evil to fruition, but this cauldron is also the mother of our salvation and where we, the church, exist to be the ambassadors of salvation along with the Holy Spirit and the blood of Christ as the agents of salvation.

Another good illustration of this temporary, formative period is to think of it as Paul did in Romans 8 (Christ uses the same metaphor in the Upper Room) as a protective period of gestation in God's creative womb. This age we have called time is indeed the cauldron and crucible in which He is permitting evil and suffering in order to birth His ultimate will, including redeemed man as his perfect companion in eternity future beyond the limits of time and space. as we currently know them, infinity. Additionally, the ideas of gestation and especially labor and birth, entail the reality of pain and suffering, but for a purpose. Both we and the creation are groaning in this expectant, gravid time as we await the glorious and full fruition of our full sonship with the Creator of the universe.

A close friend has also compared this time to a bud, pregnant with the manifold fruit of God's complete will for us and His creation. Sadly, what we see with our eyes all too often is the 'reality' of this temporary bubble or womb, forgetting we are commanded to live by faith in God's Word and promises. Real faith is looking beyond what we can see with our earthly eyes and understand with our minds and rather look with our spirits aided by God's Spirit into the true reality of the ultimate meaning of the full relationship we have and will have with Him throughout all eternity, infinity.

Micah alludes to the same with these words, *"He hath shewed thee, O man, what is good; and what doth the LORD require of thee, but to do justly, and to love mercy, and to walk humbly with thy God."* It is only in this that we can survive the hurts, trials and cruelties of this life and indeed even find joy in them and by His grace even grow more like His Son in them until He calls us home to exist in unity and eternity with Him. Indeed, the full realization of this has been of immense help for me in my dealing with the grief in the death of my wife, son and 4-month-old grandson in succession.

In Philippians 2, Paul writes of Christ leaving the glory of heaven; and in humility in the incarnation, He not only took on our flesh but also came to live within His own creation to be confined by time and space, the finite. His mission was to become fully one of us and to live with us so that He could die for us bringing us our salvation with its immediate regeneration of the spirit and ultimate glorification in the life outside of our decaying bodies. Occupying new bodies, as is His, never again to be confined by time and space and forever living in the regenerated universe and discovering its mysteries and ruling with Him over it. In other words, the incarnation of Christ begets the glorification of His body and His beloved bride, His church, destined to be forever one with Him and a part of Him in sharing His divinity, including His infinity.

In this, God has turned our lives, dead in sin and limited by the cold, ultimate finiteness of death, into the reality of glorious, eternal life in which He will share His infinite nature with us. Infinite in length. Infinite in presence. Infinite in knowledge, and infinite in love. The word infinite, even in its broadest and deepest and widest and longest sense in time, cannot accurately and fully describe the nature of the future (also tainted by the finite) life because there is a sense of scale in it. In the new reality, we and the creation will be transported beyond and out of our current reality, framed by time and space. The visible (our temporal reality) will be swallowed up by the invisible (God's overarching reality).

Let's consider the concept of knowledge again. Recently, one night, I was working on my family tree genealogy while preparing to sleep. In this process, my iPad froze, so I had to reboot it, and in doing so I had the opportunity of seeing and thus considering the Apple icon: The metaphorical apple representing the possession, analysis and communication of knowledge with its bite (visual pun on byte) having been taken by a user, clever indeed.

I returned to my work for an hour or so and finally stopped in favor of prayer and sleep. I thought of a prayer topic and with none coming to mind, I simply asked my Father what He wanted to pray about with me. (I consider prayer a conversation.) He quickly brought to mind the tree of the knowledge of good and evil, which grew in the original Garden, and from which Adam and Eve were forbidden to partake of its fruit, apples. This fruit of this tree of course if eaten would impart the knowledge of good, in its loftiest ideals, the beautiful virtues God which in His love has now gifted through His Holy Spirit, and of evil in its deepest, ugliest and blackest aspects devised in the heart of Satan and fallen man, from which God has redeemed us. Omniscience and prescience were to be reserved for God in the Garden.

However, paradoxically, man and woman, through their presumptuous sin, attempted to steal from God that which He planned to give them all along and ironically did legally through their sin and in Christ's taking on that sin and the punishment for it on the cross. Peter instructs that God, through His great and precious promises, has made the church, the body and bride of Christ, partakers of His divine nature: At least in part omniscience and immortality in the life to come. As Paul put it—we will know as we are known. Even Confucius wrote 2500 years ago that learning should never cease, as knowledge is infinite. Martin Luther King spoke of the arc of the moral universe as infinite, and it bends (by God) toward justice—His perfect knowledge and application of His law mixed with His grace in our existence.

If God imparts His knowledge to us, what shall we do with this great and precious promise but explore the infinities of both the micro and macro universe within the infinity of eternity. Ruling over the creation and being God's children and perfect companions were His plan for us from the beginning. My son, David, wrote, as previously noted, this beautiful and insightful missive on numbers (his verbalization of the creation) when he was in high school:

"Numbers can dance. I discovered the dance while preparing for the state math contest in geometry. Although the dance starts chaotically with unwieldy problems, order descends as the values interact and force themselves into patterns that settle into place. New quantities and rules emerge, enhancing the dance and making it more elaborate. After viewing the dance, I now choreograph it. Adding new rules and problems, I watch the dancers create new patterns, and I discover the dance's fundamental nature. These discoveries draw me deeper into the dance's engaging beat. I delight in the dance."

He noted that in the solving of complex geometric problems which could be grossly approached by applying rote formulas, it became much easier and more engaging to get to watch the dance take him progressively from the one dimensional (linear) to the two (area) and three (space) dimensional and even beyond into the heart of God's dance of infinity beyond dimensions including time. There, I think, he encountered God and was taken beyond the confines of our earthly reality as was I while facing death in the car, Isaiah in the temple and Paul on the road trip to Damascus, that is into infinity.

David's words and thoughts are a beautiful metaphor restating what Einstein theorized mathematically in his theories of relativity: That is, time and space are not fixed in nature but change or even cease to exist on the fringes of our know reality. That time and space are relative are now known as empiric facts, as both change with the effects of velocity and gravity. If our reality here is changeable, might it not exist at all in God's infinity?

Is the dance not the love and knowledge of our Father, and is the beat of the dance not the heartbeat of God calling and drawing His beloved into His bosom of relationship and His work for us? Will we heed His call, and will we delight in Him and dance before Him and with Him, as did King David?

Christ was offering a similar concept in demonstrating and living within the infinite in declaring himself to be our alpha and omega and with the seven 'I Am' statements recorded in John. He is really declaring that He, alone, is the door to the infinite life not only in eternity but also the learning of it and practice of it in this finite earthly life, a contradiction but nevertheless true.

Paul refers to this in Phil. 2 as the working out of our salvation in following the example of Christ in the giving up of our lives in obedience, humility and sacrifice for others as did our Lord for us. This concept is also depicted by Christ in His stating we must give up our old (finite) lives and die to them in the grave of His spiritual baptism so that we can be raised into a new (infinite) life. This sacrifice of our lives in the moment of our regeneration and in its day-to-day practice on the altar of God is pleasing to Him as we become more like His Son in our sanctification (Romans 12:1-2).

All too often in this life, we allow ourselves to be paralyzed in our walk with God by our own selflessness and inhibitions and the traditions and legalisms that others would foist upon us (propositional prisons rather than real) and all of which rob us of the opportunity to bless others and be blessed ourselves and thus of pursuing the infinite.

As an example, consider how the pursuit of comfort and subtle or overt greed but even more often the Old Testament idea of tithing prevents the blessings for the potential cheerful giver in 2 Corinthians 9. God loves His children in whom He can invest more and more of His Kingdom resources to be reinvested in the lives of others, with the givers becoming fountains of blessing.

This never occurs in its fullest capacity with linear thinking but only with infinity type thinking empowered by the Holy Spirit and by escaping from the shackles of the thinking of our artificial prisons, which are even sometimes begotten of church or denominational tradition. God does not want us to act in a predictable pattern or a repeating recipe or by our man-made creeds, but always in the infinite thinking of faith.

After God saved my life in the accident chronicled above, I determined I would never again allow the God-given days of my life to fall fruitless and dead to the cold, hard ground. Rather, I firmly determined I would, to the best of my ability, use my God-given days and talents to enhance the lives of my family, friends, patients, co-workers and the lost and hurting and be a blessing to them and thus bring a blessing to me as well. This has often required non-linear thought and action and always intentional effort.

I only use the example of Ruth and me as an expedient and proximate and convenient example in our giving above and beyond with others in His Bethany House ministry in the rescuing and restoration of women, addicted to drugs, and secondarily to their families, thus hopefully breaking the generational cycle. We have witnessed the miraculous and healing and infinite power of God at work indeed!

The most remarkable event of blessing occurred to me on this very day as I began to write this missive, which was set into motion by an act of kindness on my part thirty years ago.

A late middle-aged couple were traveling through Clarksville when the husband developed a critical illness and died under my care at the hospital despite our best efforts, including emergent surgery.

I found myself in our ICU waiting room with his grieving and devastated wife. I related the facts and was as compassionate as I could be, and the time came for my departure. I was torn between offering to take her home with me out of compassionate concern and constrained by my inhibitions and propriety. Thank God I listened to Him in my heart and acted outside of the box and took her home, where my wife and I gave her the love of God in assisting her and helping make arrangements for the next day.

It was a blessing, not only for her but for Melynda and me also, and it became even more so for me three months later as we shared our mutual grief by phone and letter when Melynda died herself. And we surmised God had inexorably and forever weaved our lives together in this life and in infinity. We just never know how God will take our day-by-day acts of faith and exponentially multiply them as my David envisioned by his understanding of God's ways through his insight and participation in the dance of numbers from the linear to infinity.

My faith would take me to the infinity of trust in God, but my flesh and my prisons would hold me back, and I certainly have had my struggles of faith amid my trials and tribulations, but by His grace, I possess His joy and live in His purpose with overcoming endurance in giving my life as best I can in obedience, service and sacrifice to Him.

To state again, today, just as I sat down to write this missive while at my desk having lunch, I opened a piece of mail, which turned out to be a powerful 'thank you' note:

"Dr. Carrigan, I am DC, and I am writing to let you know that my mother, FMD, passed away recently. I want to thank you for your act of kindness 30 years ago when my father died there. Your act made our grief bearable and has marked the rest of our lives. So, thank you so much."

DC probably does not know or remember that God's intervening in our collective lives had everything to do with my surviving and overcoming in my grief in Melynda's death just three months later. You see, the giving of oneself almost always comes back from God as a blessing multiplied many times and lasting over many years in this life, and will be preserved and enjoyed forever in eternity as the taste of a fine wine lingers and as the glow of an embrace and kiss of a loved one warms the heart in remembrance.

I close with this wonderful metaphor. Some weeks after David died, I asked God for a sign of comfort. Two nights later, as I was attempting to work at the computer in the wee hours of the morning, I was distracted by a curious, small moth attempting to find his way from the darkness of the night into the warm and inviting light of my screen. I tried to swat him away a few times, but he was persistent in his trials. Out of frustration, I successfully captured him in my cupped hands, and he frantically tried to escape, perhaps in fear and desperation, being surrounded by the black finiteness of his apparent impending death. But I was able to let him escape into the freedom of the backyard as I opened my hands and gently threw him out into his new abode. The Holy Spirit immediately imparted to me the comfort of knowing it was the same with God and David. He struggled with the trials, hurts and darkness of life and was searching for light and comfort, and finally, his Father took him into the safety of His mighty hands. For a brief time, perhaps, death seemed as a black, empty, eternal tomb to him. But, oh, the thrill when he realized God's hands did not take a dark tomb form, but rather a soft cocoon from which he emerged into the glory and all the infinities of eternal life.

Thus, living in the infinity of heaven will be a sure reality, but the question then becomes, will we allow God to teach us of and lead us into the infinite 'heavenly things' here in this finite life or will we not? The choice is our own and on those daily choices depends on the blessings God would give to us and others through us and thus how infinite our lives can become in demonstrating God's love to others and in our own sanctification.

As a closing thought, I add the following poem begun by my David and finished by me after his passing. It speaks of God's bridging our souls from the turmoil and suffering of this finite life and beyond our unreachable horizons to the infinity of His perfect will for us. Even better, we have the ability with His aid to begin this journey with Him into infinity at this very minute if we only choose to do so.

Life and Death and Glory

The tide ever ebbs low
Pulling my soul into the stormy sea,
Erstwhile taking my dreams and will
From my heart and being.
Thus, stealing painful tears for itself from me.

A slither of a moon rides high in the sky,
Its rays of sharp light piercing through my soul
Passing into the cool, white sand,
And reflecting the emptiness of my heart,
Which itself is devoid of light and feeling.

The mighty, relentless waves and wind
Pound against my mind
Ever eroding and changing me
Into small grains of salty sand
Blown across the beach and claimed for itself.

Now death itself
Has posted its claim against me.
I cannot myself see beyond its dark curtain
Or the hazy horizon of the tide and sea
Or even the moon's menacing realm.

What can save me

From nature's onslaught, my enemy?

It appears only an unknown supernatural power.

I know no such force.

I only know my God!

The prophet questioned God of His justice.

"The just shall live by faith."

"Though the fig tree shall not blossom

And the crops die,

I will only trust in my God."

The weeping prophet declared the same.

"God, you have abandoned me in the pit!"

"Take heart as I have called you,

And I will deliver you."

I will only believe in my God.

I plead with my brother, Paul,

"Who will deliver me

From this body of death?

Only through Jesus Christ, my Lord!"

I will always thank my God.

Life itself and death have stolen my being.

I could not save myself from either.

God has bridged both my flaws and all horizons,

And has glorified me by taking me into Himself.

I now declare with Job,

"I know my Redeemer liveth!"

Of Sanctification–Personal Application

In putting the concepts, necessities and the imperative of Philippians 2, Romans 12 and Matthew 10:39 into effect in our lives, what must we do?

What did I do?

First, we must realize our lives belong to God and are not our own.

Second, the process of sanctification is lifelong. Just as an infant is not born as a mature adult, newly converted Christians must be discipled and nurtured into maturity. The basic Christian doctrines and practices must be mastered and built upon as the writer of Hebrews suggests in chapter six.

How is this done? Bible study, mentorship and accountability and discipline, if necessary, prayer, fellowship and the guidance of the Holy Spirit. All of this was provided to me by my parents, Melynda and faithful others in my walk and continues to this day.

The nature of our prayers even changes as we mature. It seems many immature Christians petition God regarding wants and needs in attempting to change His will to theirs. This is certainly biblical, as God our Father wants the best for us, His beloved children.

A higher form of prayer is the reverse in praying God's will be done on Earth as it is in heaven as our Lord instructed in His model prayer for us.

There is, however, a still higher form of prayer, in which we become one with God, as Christ himself prayed in the upper room. These episodes are epiphanies in the Christian life and become a window into our relationship with Him in eternity. They are also almost always nonverbal, totally on a spiritual plain mixed with the blood of Jesus and empowered by the Holy Spirit, a rehearsal for heaven even.

Here, our wills are briefly joined in unity with His in a mysterious, miraculous and marvelous way. Our wants and needs melt as snow in the warm sun in these moments and we can truly pray, "Thy will be done!"

It was certainly like this for me, as I explained in the moment of unity with God when I thought I was dying. We must remember we humans are constantly dying.

From our perspective, the process is not always evenly paced or linear, but by sudden change. Our lives in the various spheres (spiritual, marital, social, professional) are stable for significant periods interrupted by abrupt crises or decision points which take us out of one stable stage into another.

God calls, and if we listen, we, in faith, follow.

Such was the case in my life just before I was 50 at Thanksgiving in 2000. Ruth and our family had enjoyed thirteen stable years after Melynda's death. God had already called us back to church through certain events and friendships, but we were about to enter a new era, at first out of sight and beyond our comprehension.

I had read the Gospel of John many times prior to that time, but the Holy Spirit this time spoke to me differently, unction and calling. I realized as I knew God more deeply and understood the plight of my fellow man more sympathetically and empathetically, I would then be drawn to live with both God and fellow man more earnestly and sincerely.

This was before I understood the calling of Philippians 2 and Romans 12. But from the above, thoughts flowed the notion of obedience and service and sacrifice, and the idea of finding deeper and more meaningful life by giving it away to others.

Finally, the Spirit promised if I did this, others would be saved and richly blessed as would I. This promise has been beautifully fulfilled many times over.

I was unaware until just after that our pastors and congregation were preparing to go on a mission. One must go beyond verse 2 of Romans 12 to learn this process is not for the individual but is a work of the corporate body of Christ melding miraculously and mightily the various gifts and strengths and weaknesses of the church.

It was a wondrous work of partnership missions.

We soon began going to the slums of Rio de Janeiro and the farms and cities of China, 22 times in all, for me. For my family, this was a life-changing series of events: Lives touched, souls saved, hope restored.

China I was blessed with the opportunity to share my faith with a group of chef students.

I, "it was a pleasure caring for your physical needs and sicknesses just now. But do you know, you also have spiritual illnesses which will lead to spiritual death?"

One young man in the back is enthusiastically assenting and agreeing in gesticulation and verbally in Chinese. At the same time, 2–3 others arise and leave.

"Just as I have a cure for physical illness, I can also tell you of a cure for the disease of sin and disobedience of the God who created you can provide."

More vigorous approval and more leave.

"Because of your sin, you will always be separated from God, your Father. The cure is that God sent His own Son, Jesus, to take your sin and my sin upon Himself, and found guilty by His Father was punished by dying on a cross, spilling His blood for our salvation, justification and redemption and thus, eternal life with God."

More excitement and more leave.

"So, then your salvation is a matter of grace and is a free gift, to accept in praying to God for forgiveness and restoration. If you want us to help you pray that prayer, come down and join us."

Many do while others leave as the young man approaches me, broadly smiling.

Believing he must already be a Christian, I ask, "Are you a Christian?"

"Not until now!"

"Not until now."

We welcomed him as a new Christian brother.

Where is he now? What has his walk been like? Is he growing?

I don't know, but I look forward to knowing in heaven and meeting him again.

These experiences had a profound effect on all our lives: Both the proclaimers and the receivers, and we are all a part of the body of Christ.

I could go on and on but will leave you with this special story, also from China. It speaks for itself.

"It is September 6, 2006, and I find myself on my third medical mission trip to China with my wife and three dear friends and fellow travelers. Today, we have ministered to the people of JD, a very remote village in time, society and spirit.

Indescribable and unimaginable trash, filth, poverty, and illness abound as we care for the imprisoned, oppressed souls who live there in a dark pagan temple made of wood with dirt floors. A higher official is angry with the local leader because he has allowed foreigners into the village without the official's knowledge. And so, it miserably and endlessly goes on and on and on.

In my quiet time following lunch, I am compelled to pray that God will loosen the bonds with which they have been enslaved by Satan and his minions.

As we return to our 'home' that afternoon, the Holy Spirit begins to speak to me and enlighten me through my recent studies in Hebrews and Henry Drummond's, The Programme of Christianity, which I am continuing to read on the bus. He eloquently writes of human suffering and sorrow, which come not so much from the way men die but from the way they live and are forced to live. He further states some men live and exist in hellish prisons, where no breath of heaven ever reaches and where social soils exist in which only sin and unrighteousness can grow and flourish. He declares these systems must be destroyed, and the captives set free!

Moreover, he opines that wherever the poor are trodden upon or tread upon each other; wherever the air is poison and the water foul; wherever want stares at us, and vice reigns, and rags rot—there is where the Avenger (God and His arm, The Church) must take its stand.

One of my spiritual mentors, who handed me the book as we were leaving on our trip, wrote in the margin of this very page that my (our) imminent challenge and calling are the above thoughts. And indeed, they are the urgent and clarion call of our Lord to His Church today. Do we hear? Do we understand? Will our hearts be stirred? Will we act!

This evening, my friends and I have the privilege of meeting and speaking with a Chinese pastor, a truly first century type, Holy Spirit inspired preacher and man of God. He ministers in an unregistered house church and shares with us the stories of his church's trials, tribulations, and personal persecutions.

The authorities have already threatened to close the Sunday School but were thwarted by the Holy Spirit's miraculous intervention in confusing and thus preventing the children from identifying their teachers.

The pastor was detained, questioned, threatened and forbidden to hold further open assemblies and evangelize. Under this pressure, the Holy Spirit gave him courage and the faith to both verbally refuse and to refuse signing a paper promising the same. We could see the light of the Holy Spirit in his countenance as he related this story. Paul and Silas must have looked the same as they walked out of their prison!

Despite all this, the congregation spiritually flourishes and has grown to several thousand members, but now must break up into several hundred cells and have the daunting task of training hundreds of new leaders.

One must ask, how does the present-day church in America compare with this shining example? It seems we build cathedrals and our personal barns and study theories of theology and worship; but our buildings are cold and there is too little empathy for the lost and little true worship and joy in our hearts as we rest in our artificial comfort.

And the God given days of opportunity in our lives slip away one by one just as the dead leaves of autumn fall from fruitless trees to the cold, hard ground.

The writer of Hebrews instructs us to move beyond our complacency and the foundational tenets of our faith and thus begin using the Gospel as the daily signpost of our lives. He also challenges us to leave our milk behind and to eat the meat of evangelism and discipleship in these last days. I praise God that He has placed my family in an outward focused, mission minded church such as First Baptist, which is one of the bright lights in the firmament of the Body of Christ.

May we remain diligent in finishing the race our Lord has set before us so that when He returns, He will say, "Well done, my good and faithful servants." Let us continue to keep in step with God's program and together march by faith into His new frontier of missions and with the Holy Spirit be the Avenger of the poor and lost."

I now sense that our God is again calling us into the realities and fullness of Philippians 2 and Romans 12.

Will we hear?

Will we be obedient?

Will we follow?

PS:

I offer this poem, explaining the song from deep within our hearts:

Where the Sirens Sing

Life, the perfect gift of God,

Presented as perfectly pristine,

And enormously inviting.

No compass or roadmap provided.

Friends, family

And the eddies and currents of life,

Day by day,

And the tides' ebbing and flowing,

Season by season,

Carry from shore to shore.

Love, joy and peace,

Hurt, pain and grief,

All flow in and out

Forever chiseling and changing us,

For both good and bad,

Better or worse.

Some find anchor on solid rock,

Others on shifting sand,

Some safe harbor in Faith, Hope and Love,

While others drift on the waves

As solitary gulls isolated in lonely misery.

Some excel and grow,

Others fall behind and shrivel.

Some are nurtured

While others abused.

While all along,

Deep inside ourselves,

In the primal mists of our souls,

Where secret, sacred sirens sing the song,

We must all follow in life

Until death calls us into tomorrow.

Of Jacob and Israel
Old Testament Sanctification

Have you ever studied and wondered about the life of Jacob? I have because I am so much like him. He was close to his mother, intelligent, self-reliant, a trickster and independent. He, with the assistance of his mother, stole his brother's birthright and the blessing of his father, and then fled undercover in the middle the night to Bethel, where on the first night of his journey, he used a pile of rocks for a pillow. I was much the same my first night away from home, beginning medical school.

It was there he saw the ladder into heaven with the Lord reaffirming His Blessing and protection, just as I perceived it God's will in my becoming a doctor.

He then proceeded to his uncle Laban's farm, where he was tricked into marrying Leah by Laban, then Rachael after seven more years' work. It might be thought by some that this marrying of Leah was a huge mistake, but consider, Leah was the ancestor of Jesus, not Rachael.

How often do God's plans trump ours? Often, to be sure!

Master trickster vs. master trickster, Jacob vs. Laban.

Jacob also became the world's first genetic engineer in breeding cattle of his kind to his ownership rather than his uncle's. So, after several generations, he owned virtually all the cattle; and once again, he left in the middle of the night with his family and cattle.

His ingenuity now had placed Jacob in a vice, closing in physically between Laban left behind and Esau ahead, with God enclosing spiritually on all fronts. A trapped man.

Peace made with Laban, he proceeded warily toward his brother, ultimately hiding behind trees as a coward while sending family and friends ahead.

That night, he encountered the Lord and wrestled in vain throughout the night, and he was finally broken physically in his hip and spiritually broken in life.

A changed man, from scheming and self-reliance to a man of faith.

A changed name, from Jacob to Israel.

A form of Old Testament salvation and sanctification.

In my own life, I've been so much like Jacob. As physicians, we are educated and trained to be so. In facing life and death medical situations, one must learn to act prudently, quickly and independently, or a life could be lost unnecessarily. In fact, most physicians are innately turned toward independent thinking, and this trait is honed to a fine, sharp point in medical school and training and by experience.

The conundrum then becomes this fierce independence does not at all lend itself to the contexts of family, friends and church, where interdependence and unity are so important. Many physicians really struggle here. I know I do, and most likely always will, to an extent.

I pray my friends and Christian brothers understand. I know my wife does as she is a nurse and has seen me in emergent actions many times. I also pray that as I continue the trail of sanctification, God will continue to love and guide me.

I know He will!

At some point, we must all be broken, or cease growing.

WHO SHALL SPEAK?

Who shall speak to me,

Of things to come,

Of things to be,

The pinnacle of mind,

The height of heart,

For life, a beautiful melody?

Who shall speak,

Of the beauty of art,

In the soft note of a poem,

Or of simple delight of another day,

As life is shared

Along its way?

Who shall speak,

Of verdant, fertile field,

At once lovely,

And advancing life,

Or of cloudy, serene sunset

Plaid colors blown on the wind?

Who shall speak,

Of tender maternal smile

For newborn babe,

Or of father teaching son

Of strength of thought

And virtues of life,

For which some count for naught?

Who will speak,

And lead us to know

That the care we show

And respect we sow

Are so much more

Than being right

And always in the know?

Who will speak the truth?

That who we are

And who we may together be

Is so much more profound

Than who I am

And how my dogma sounds!

Who shall speak to me,

Of things to come,

Of things to be,

The pinnacle of mind,

The height of heart,

For life, a beautiful melody?

OF THE BETHANY HOUSE

The Bethany House opened in TN in March 2013 in my ancestral farm home several months after my nephew tragically died there of an accidental drug overdose.

A graduate's, MK, message of thanks on my birthday:

"Happy Birthday to my adopted father, I can't begin to express the gratefulness I have for you Dr. Mike Carrigan, you saw something in me that I never would have without you! I love you so very much and my life will be forever impacted because of you! I hope you have the best birthday ever!"

Many years before, my first cousin, RD, had established the first BH in GA, then moving to AL on her farm. While visiting me with one of her recent graduates, KC, who was her then current director.

They, "Mike, what are you going to do with the farmhouse?"

"I don't know. Why?"

"Well, we were thinking about starting BH 2 there. What do you think?"

I asked, "When do we start?"

We quickly developed a plan, budget and found a director, KT, a graduate herself. We marshaled the support of many individuals and churches. We, at first, were doubted by some, but some became integrated into and trusted by the community.

The ministry was designed as a Jesus based, nine-month in-residence program designed for salvation from sin and restoration of life for drug-addicted women. There was no cost for the 'students'. Many of them were in the legal system and came as an alternative to jail or prison. Almost all were deeply estranged from family, friends and outcasts from society, most also totally hopeless.

One of the first five was JR whom you met in the chapter on community. She was 30 and had been raised in a bi-vocational pastor's home who had died suddenly of a heart attack when she was 19. This, and friction with her mother, sent her out of control into the abyss of sin and drugs. She had hit the bottom when she came to TN from GA.

From the beginning, she seemed engaged, but on a special night in early summer, I got the first true glimpse of the power of God at work in her heart and in the ministry. It was the occasion of our Sunday School picnic at the farmhouse. She walked slowly out the back door onto the deck and asked for attention.

"I want to give you my life story," she haltingly announced. All eyes turn expectantly to her.

She told of her father's death and of living in the streets; helpless and hopeless, addicted. She continued, "I came to TN to find God, and I have in this place. I am so thankful. I have never sung before, but God has given me that gift. I want to sing for you. Oh, Lord my God, when I in awesome wonder ... How great thou art. How great thou art!"

Acapella and marvelous, and not a dry eye present as we were witnessing a miracle.

JR recorded a few songs informally, beautifully and wonderfully used her newly discovered her in her testimony.

She graduated on schedule and was married shortly thereafter. She asked me to stand in as her father to give her away.

In front of the Hickory Point church while awaiting the bridal processional, I told her, "Jessie, your earthly father is dead, and you have a heavenly Father. If you will have me, from this day forward, I am now your father and you, my daughter."

And so, we are.

By June, she was reunited with her three daughters, twins aged eight and the oldest fifteen. When David died, they were visiting her. At the service at FBC, we had already sung 'All Is Well with My Soul', and I had eulogized my son.

Near the end, Jessie came to sing 'How Great Thou Art' at my request. She broke down and began crying amid the last verse. Her until recently estranged daughter came and embraced her and as they cried together, the congregants stood and finished the praise together.

What a scene!

What a testimony!

Some months later, KT resigned, and Jessie and family came to the house as she assumed the directorship, performing in a stellar and faithful manner, truly a genius in balancing love and instruction with discipline and accountability,

She poured out her life there for three years with about twelve graduates, all of whom are, as she, are doing well, reunited with families and employed.

The testimony of one of her early graduates, LN:

"This is my story of brokenness, heartbreak, loss, hopelessness, depression, inadequacies, abuse, self-loathing, self-destruction, and addiction, but this story is not a tragedy. This is a 'Come Back' story with an ending I never saw coming. It was not until I had lost everything that I loved I found everything I needed. It was not until my back was against the wall and I was facing what seemed like insurmountable odds, in the basement of rock bottom, that I had dug with my bare hands, that I found my hope. Jesus was my

hope. He had been there patiently waiting for me all along. This is a love story, and it has a happy ending.

I have gone to church my whole life and came to know Jesus as my Savior when I was nine years old. I had a close relationship with Him until I reached my early twenties, when I began straying from the path God had set for me. Perhaps it was my stubborn and rebellious ways that had started my falling away from the right path, but unannounced to me, a car crash in December 2009 would leave me with a serious back injury and a future dependence and addiction to prescription pain medications that would take my life and help me destroy everything I loved. I was married to the love of my life, and I had two beautiful children, but there was a deep heaviness that would ache inside me. There was a brokenness I could not comprehend, and the more I tried to ignore that ache, the more my life fell apart. I was powerless to stop it.

My husband had become verbally, mentally, and emotionally abusive, constantly bombarding me with fierce and malicious words that broke me down until I believed the hate he said to me. I believed him when he told me I was not good enough, that I was ugly, that I was fat, that I was not loved, that I was the reason he had multiple affairs. I used the pain medication to numb my broken heart and to silence the torturous thoughts of my inadequacies, low self-esteem, low self-worth, and self-loathing that constantly haunted me.

Over the next two years, my addiction became so severe that I would lie, cheat, and steal from anyone to get whatever pill I could to have just a moment of relief from the hell I called life. It was not until after getting a DUI, a halfhearted attempt at rehab, the possibility of going to jail for a probation violation, the dissolution of my marriage, my mother blocking my phone number, and my children needing to be protected from me, I knew I had a problem.

I can vividly remember feeling so broken and so defeated that no matter how much I used, I felt nothing. I was already dead inside and did not care if my body followed in death. It was in this moment of complete and utter hopelessness that God sent an angel to rescue me, and I unequivocally surrendered to Him. He had been there waiting for me for years, not to guilt, shame, or condemn me, but to say, "Come here, welcome home, I love you".

I had destroyed my life, but God had given me a peace and a strength that I have never encountered before, and day by day He was restoring what I had destroyed. When I finally got out of the driver's seat, got in the trunk of the car, and gave the steering wheel of my life back to God, my recovery became the easiest hard thing I had ever done.

Christ did not give me my old life back, but instead, He delivered me from despair and gave me a whole new life. I no longer look to the world to define my worth; I am a daughter of the Creator of the Universe; I know my worth. If I were the only person in the world who needed salvation, God would have still sent his son, Jesus, to die for me! I am that worthy, loved, cherished, admired, cared for, and worth dying for; and I live for His acceptance and love. That love saved me at Calvary, saved me from myself, and continues to save me every single day that He gives me strength to fight my addiction.

I have learned that all this makes me fragile, fierce, clever, powerful, wounded, creative, layered, thoughtful, moody, insightful, wild, and damaged, can be described as lovely and in His image. I do not want to miss out on experiencing all He has for me, because I am afraid of the dark, and the deep, the unknown.

Every time I have let go of the need to control, and stepped out and away from the safety and comfort I could sense was holding me back, He has rewarded me and shown me His favor.

Every time I have pushed through fear, my faith has been taken to the next level, and I have been able to accomplish what I never thought possible. God is calling us into the deep. He wants to dazzle us, and that is where the magic happens.

But He also wants us to show Him we really, really want it, and are willing to swim out away from the safety of the shore to get it. This, to me, is childlike faith and what I strive for everyday."

I can certainly add nothing to such a story.

Another of Jessie's graduates, HS:

"Dr. Mike Carrigan, this has truly been an amazing journey for me. I'm so grateful God sent me here to the Bethany House ... God knew before I knew that this was where I needed to be to wholeheartedly gain my strength, love, and knowledge of his word. I have learned so much through this program, from God speaking through You, Mrs. Ruth, Mrs. Jessie, and Mr. Ron and all the other godly people he has placed in my life. I have felt love from each and every one who is a part of this ministry. No one has judged me for my wrong doings but encouraged me each day to strive to be more Christ-like. Even though I went through a rough patch in life, God was always there, and He knew where it would lead me ... So, I'm grateful for the trials and sufferings because it has brought me back to God. I look at my rough patch as a blessing now ... Thank you for opening this ministry ... God is here working daily, and I'm beyond blessed to get to be a part of the Bethany House and to learn and to see God working in not only my life but everyone's life who is a part of this ministry. Thank you for everything you guys have and are doing for me and all the ladies who come through here ... I've been blessed with this amazing opportunity. I'm glad this was part of God's will for my life because I've added onto my family, and I have gained some incredible Godly people.

Love Always,

HS"

Certainly, no additions are needed here either.

Here is the testimony of JP, one of our early graduates:

"My name is JP, and I am 27 years old. I was raised by my mom and dad until I was four years old and then they divorced, and I found myself living in a broken home. My mom remarried. My stepfather, Ken, was the father figure most of my young life. My Dad would call me a lot ... he lived about 15 miles from me. He would say he would come pick me up for the weekend. I would sit and wait, watching each car go by, but he never showed. When he did, I never knew what might happen. I remember being shot at by an

angry woman once, left with random people, or left in rooms alone with other kids or by myself for hours while my dad was in another room.

All throughout elementary and middle school, I never fit in anywhere. I didn't make a lot of friends, and I felt like an outcast. I was different.

My mother was always totally consumed with their business, and it left little time for me. My stepfather wasn't very nice to me at all. He never physically abused me; it was emotional abuse.

We went to church a lot, and I had a lot of knowledge about God, but I had no idea who He was.

Because of my stepdad's job, we moved around a lot. I was really scared when we moved to GA in 6th grade. That is when I met the friends I've carried throughout my life. I didn't feel like I completely fit in, but this was by far the closest friends I had ever had. In high school, I became the class clown, drowning in my insecurities. I smoked marijuana at the age of 15. During that year, I met D. He was the first guy to take interest in me, and soon, we were inseparable. I became pregnant, but had a miscarriage early on. Very soon after that, I became pregnant with T. I was 16. It was not acceptable with my family to be pregnant so young and especially unmarried. During my pregnancy, my stepfather died of a massive heart attack. I don't remember many things from my childhood, and I have tried to block it out completely. When T was born, I thought to myself, I had never seen such a beautiful baby in all my life.

Not long after that, I first experimented with meth. I only used a handful of times. I was introduced to it by D's mother. When T was three months old, I started school for cosmetology. My grandparents paid for daycare, and with a lot of family support, I graduated in 2005. Soon after, I started working in my first hair salon and caught on really quick. Mine and D's relationship had become sour, and we fought a lot. Soon, it became downright unhealthy. I was a victim of domestic violence. Almost every morning, he got mad and went off the deep end. I was so embarrassed and ashamed to be allowing this to happen to me. I never told anyone because I knew I deserved it, after all,

I'm the one who kept coming back. I desperately wanted out, and I wept and prayed every night for God to give me the strength to get away.

All these years, I saw my dad a lot, and he came to live with me on and off, but I had no respect for him, and we usually ended up yelling at each other and parted ways for months at a time. D and I were on and off for a couple of years, when we found out I was pregnant again! And it was going to be a BOY! When he was born, I didn't think I could love another human being as much as I did T, but he was so precious, and I realized I loved both more than life itself.

When B was only three months old, D told me he was leaving me for one of my very best friends. Eventually he cut ties with me and married her. This rocked my world. Even though we had a bad relationship, he was all I knew. Our mothers helped me out a lot, it was like a blur, and the next part of my life consisted of working, struggling to pay my bills, provide for my children, try to be a good mother and all the while smoking marijuana and being very promiscuous.

Now I can see D leaving was the answer to my prayers, but I was as lost as ever. I was still searching for something that seemed I would never find. I didn't even know where to look. I surrounded myself with people day and night. I hated being alone, and I sought company at all costs. I bought people groceries, and I gave rides and gas money away, whatever it took to keep them coming around.

Now, looking back, I see the patterns of co-dependence in my life. This is when I met R ... I thought he was the love of my life. He was the funniest, smartest, kindest person I had ever met, and seemed to love me just the way I was. He had such a free spirit! When we were together, I felt like I had found what I was looking for. He promised to never leave me, and I believed him. He never hit me or called me names. But before long, we began doing meth together. He had been clean for less than a year, but when he picked it up, I was more than willing to do it with him. I had been able to quit before. No big deal, right? This wasn't like the first few times I had ever used; it was another life. A whole new group of people and we hit it off.

I eventually started using with my dad. I became totally engulfed and within a month, I was using every chance I got. R and I broke up after three months and we didn't see each other for the next year. If I thought I was devastated from losing D, it was nothing compared to how heartbroken I was then.

I was fired from my job as a hair stylist and found a space for rent very close by. By this time, I realized I had a true talent for doing hair, and I had acquired a lot of clients. Thus, with my grandparents' help, I opened my very own hair salon, it was called 'Hair Fanatic'.

I was doing meth frequently. On the day of my grand opening, R came to see the shop, and he walked back into my life. We moved in together, my addiction deepened; and where I was a functioning addict before, I became less and less functional. I tried to blame everything and everyone for the position I had gotten myself into. I was so bitter. As I spent more and more money on the drugs, I paid less and less on the bills. I used meth every day for almost two years, and I didn't like that I had a hard time making it through the day without it.

I decided to move out of my house. The children went to live with my mom. She said they could stay with her until I got back on my feet. I actually lived in my shop for about a month, but finally decided I needed to close it down. In a way, it was freeing, because now I didn't have to spend all day trying to pretend I wasn't high. For the next year, I jumped from house to house, filling deeper and deeper with guilt and shame for not being there for my children, but still not addressing my responsibilities.

It was a daily battle within myself. I constantly tried to fill a void that I couldn't fill with drugs. I had wanted to quit for so long. I knew this wasn't how I wanted to live my life, but I just couldn't completely quit. My life was totally out of control. On Oct. 7th, I received a phone call that would change my life forever. Although I hadn't spoken to R for almost six months, he consumed my daily thoughts. I can't put into words what it felt like when they told me he was dead. He was pulled over and, in a panic, he swallowed his drugs, and it killed him hours later in jail. I was in a state of disbelief. Drugs couldn't numb this pain, as I had tried everything.

I was more lost than ever, and I had nowhere to go, I had worn out all my welcomes. It was at this point I know God started to direct me and fill me with courage through his Holy Spirit. One day, out of the blue, I decided I was done. I didn't intend to go home and tell on myself. I thought I could change on my own, but when I started talking to my mom, everything just came out. I agreed I needed to go to rehab.

On November 30th, 2012, I went to Alabama to a place called The Bethany House. As I unchained the cattle gate, I could feel my own chains beginning to loosen. I was consumed with the presence of my Heavenly Father like I had never felt before. This began not just a program, but a new way of thinking and a new way of life. I began to learn what a relationship with God meant and as I sought Him, He drew closer to me. I finally found the only thing that could fill that void, Jesus Christ.

Towards the end of my program after moving to the Tennessee house, I was asked to go to China to cut hair on a medical mission trip. I had no money, and it was expensive, but do you know, The Lord miraculously provided that money anonymously through several doners. That was a trip I'll never forget. I did 249 haircuts while I was there. I never knew He could use my talent for His kingdom.

After I graduated from the program, I knew God was calling me to give back to this ministry and help other women like me. Currently, I work as the director of The Bethany House in AL, and I have nine students. I am transitioning back into my children's lives more and more; I see them every weekend and lots during this summer.

He has restored so many relationships in my life. I have complete faith that He will bring us back together in his perfect timing."

Amazing, and JP is now happily married, raising a bunch of kids on a farm.

When our grandson died, our BH family surrounded us with love and prayers. We were always more blessed than imaginable by the ladies there.

In all, we cared for 50 ladies over six years with 24 graduates. In 2018, we had a triple celebration: the 140th anniversary of the farm, the 5th anniversary of the BH TN and Ruth's and my 30th anniversary. Three of our pastor friends helped us to celebrate and we again exchanged wedding vows. It was a great day as most of our graduates were there with over 50 children.

It all took place under the shade of the oak tree.

In May 2019, we graduated our last two students. One, MM, is the granddaughter of a dear pastor friend in GA. Our friendship has been God ordained from the beginning and now capped off by his granddaughter's restoration in the BH. She and her co-graduate are living in Nashville and thriving.

Literally hundreds of lives were transformed in and by the BH ministry, and I will be eternally grateful for the gift of it by God. Of all the things I've accomplished in life, I think I cherish BH above all.

To God be all the glory!

Today, Jessie lives in the farmhouse with her family and works in our medical group.

PS:

I think another symbolic story of the oak tree bears repeating here, as it meant so much to most of our ladies.

Ode to Tree

Oh, splendid trebled, star crowned tree,

What does thou life mean to me?

An anchor strong,

A beating pulse so dear,

Found within thy woody tier,

Bringing joy to my heart, so near.

Life sprung from single oaken grain

Silent lying under sheets of laden leaf(s),

And under warm, soft snow blanket lay,

There, awaiting life giving Sun-soaked ray,

Calling you forth from the fertile earth,

To be greeted there by light and rain.

Ne'er to resist your Godly call,

Stretching arms of limbs into high, blue sky

Through rain, sun and winsome wind

Unfurling bounteous bouquet

Of verdant green leaves

In praise to Him Who rules on high!

An icon of our rich, rich land

Upon this place, in watch to stand.

Work and worry,

Joy and tears;

You saw them all

Throughout the years.

Boughs of strength

As an archer's bow,

Hurling arrows from your taut, sure strings

From God's own hand

Piercing spring fresh air

As the life He brings.

Work and toil,

Tears and sweat,

Wedding vows and marriage feasts,

Lives restored to rise again;

Yes, even death

All inspired by your golden breath.

All things of earth must pass away

Yes, even you

Walked through death that day.

But, oh what mirth you brought to me,

My mighty oak, a friend for'er to be,

In my heart, my beloved' tree!

When the ladies came to the house, those who were broken before the Lord were successful and those who were not failed because they were as Jacob and still scheming and lying to God and themselves and others:

Broken

Disheveled, broken,

And spiritually blind,

No hope in the offing,

No eye for the sublime.

Lowly, meek
And physically spent,
And few friends with which
Dare she share the sorrows of life.

Sojourn in grief as black
As night;
All joy lost and forlorn
As the dew goes away in the early morn.

Heavy! Heavy! Heavy!
As a boulder pulls
Down, down, down
Ever, ever closer
To grave in the cold, dark ground.

Forever lost
And locked in the shackles of sin,
Which she can't
Even begin to understand.

See her heart;
Sense her pain.
Feel her shudder
In endless reeling refrain.

Is there any hope?
She sings aloud,
And nothing hears but
The dark, angry clouds.

We found her here
By side of life's way,
Prompted by Him
With her awhile to stay.

The Bread of Life
We shared with her,
And in her heart
We sensed a stir.
Within her soul
The Lord doth now live,
As day by day
She enjoys His peace and still.

All the world over
Dear ones like this exist;
And who need to hear
In God, there is eternal bliss.

So don't stand by
And spend your life;

Join the battle

And a blow for God: do strike!

In the giving of yourself

Will surely come,

A blessing for all,

And in your heart

A melodious sweet, new song.

OF DIVERSITY

I truly believe one of the greatest joys in life is the opportunity of meeting and making new friends, especially when they are different in some way: Culture, thought, profession, nationality or religious belief. These differences should not be seen as threatening, but as an opportunity for incremental growth by both individuals.

I have made so many friends in other cultures who have enriched my life, including my young Chinese doctor friend. We speak and encourage each other at least monthly. I clearly remember getting calls of encouragement from both China and Brazil when I was in the hospital after my accident.

Allow me to relate a story from last summer.

I was driving down Madison Street this morning and saw an African American man in a suit in the middle of the highway island where Kmart used to be. It was very warm and humid and sultry. He was holding a sign that said repent and, also referencing 2 Chronicles 7:14, the verse about the healing of our land for seeking God in prayer.

When I was approaching him and before I saw him, I was already thinking about going to the black country church the next day, which was only a couple miles from our own country church in which I was raised. But I drove by because I couldn't stop in time.

I had this compelling feeling that I should go back and thus, circled all the way around Memorial Drive and parked in the restaurant parking lot and walked across to where he was and said, "Brother, that sign looks heavy. May I hold it with you for a few minutes?"

"Well sure, come on; it is indeed heavy."

We introduced ourselves; GS is a minister from Cadiz, Kentucky. We shared and prayed for each other and our land. We determined to have lunch together later, and I believe a new godly relationship has been formed by God.

It was just a beautiful serendipitous God-given moment that I wanted to share with you, my friends, as it demonstrates the love of God for us.

As it turned out, his wife, KS, runs a local school for minority children, and I was invited for a visit. There was such a peaceful and godly presence there.

To make a long story shorter, I quickly became a donor and am now on their 501(c)3 board. It is a wonderful ministry in which I have been richly blessed.

Moral of the story: Don't be afraid to jump out of your comfort zone. There may just be a huge blessing over the horizon.

I have a fellow physician friend who is Indian and Hindu. He and his wife took Ruth and me to dinner last year. The conversation turned to religion.

This is the letter I later sent to him:

"Ruth and I really enjoyed dinner with the two of you back in November. It has taken this long for me to gather my thoughts on what I wanted to say to you and your wife. Of course, I am a Protestant Christian; however, I've never shared the sometimes-dogmatic views some Christians seem to have relative to non-Christians. Christians believe, based on scripture, that there is only one way to God and that is through Christ Jesus.

However, I've always wondered how a God could send other good people who have never known Christ to eternal punishment. It doesn't make sense for a loving God to do so. Jesus instructed in Matthew 6, in the sermon on the mount, that fruitless trees will be cast into fire, while trees which bear fruit will find an eternal reward. Christ also stated in Matthew 25 that the goats, who think they are sheep, will be cast into an eternal judgment because they have never gone out of their way to visit people in prisons and to address the world's hunger and poverty, while the sheep who think they are goats are rewarded for the same fruitfulness.

While the four of us were sharing our hearts, it became evident that we all have a compassion for the imprisoned and the impoverished people of this world; and we have put our thoughts and compassion into actions.

When I asked if you were Hindu and thus believe in multiple gods, you both verbalized, "yes", but, however, these multiple gods lead one in multiple ways to the one creator God, to paraphrase your words. To be honest, that is a thought I've never heard expressed before, and I've had to ponder and ruminate about it. I think many of my conservative, Christian brothers have missed the knowledge of the infinity of whom God really is, and thus attempt to place him into their own box which engenders a false comfort in their own hearts and separates them from the eternal comfort of understanding Him through the eyes of His other creatures who differ from them. This engenders an impoverished and imprisoned life rather than a life of privilege which many consider it to be.

After I encountered these verses in Romans 2 this morning, I knew it was time to at last write you on the subject: 'He will render to each one according to his works: to those who by patience in well-doing seek for glory and honor and immortality, he will give eternal life; but for those who are self-seeking and do not obey the truth, but obey unrighteousness, there will be wrath and fury. There will be tribulation and distress for every human being who does evil, the Jew first and also the Greek, but glory and honor and peace for everyone who does good, the Jew first and also the Greek. For God shows no partiality. But a Jew is one inwardly, and circumcision is a matter of the heart, by the Spirit, not by the letter. His praise is not from man but from God.'

Our God is certainly bigger than any of us understand, and therefore, more than one way to understand Him and to know Him and to live with Him in eternity. I know that there's much that separates us in our personal spiritual beliefs; however, we at least have reached across that great divide and have found common ground in our humanity and in our searching for God. So, thanks for being our friends and sharing life with us as we pursue our journeys."

I know this last section could be offensive to some, but in reaching people of other faiths, we must be prepared to take cultural, emotional, and spiritual steps toward them.

In doing so, almost always growth occurs and, as in this case, both parties can then begin a new journey together towards and in seeking our infinite God.

If we all endeavored to do this on a regular basis, would the world become a better and safer place? However, it seems the struggle for better understanding and action will always continue daily. Critical Race Theory is a system of thinking in achieving this better understanding, but its lessons have been banned in several states, including TN, and have been deemed unbiblical by Southern Baptist seminary presidents.

As I wrote in a letter to our local paper, I consider its tenant to lead to a better way:

'There is a Better Way'

I am a lifelong resident of this community and was educated in the local public school system, where I received a wonderful education from so many great teachers.

I am also very proud of the fact that in my 40 plus years of service in our wonderful and diverse community; I have always striven to treat each and every person and patient as my brother or sister regardless of race, ethnicity, creed, social status or sexual orientation with equality, respect and compassion.

In my opinion, the primary purpose of education is to teach young people to think critically and not the ability to regurgitate facts and certainly not the advancement of one ideology over another (indoctrination rather than education) and most certainly not the proscription or restriction of viable facts or theory (censure-ship).

I was therefore greatly dismayed when I learned that our own TN legislature has legally prohibited the teaching of Critical Race Theory in our schools.

CRT simply posits that racism systemically and institutionally exists in our culture, government, schools, work and even churches and, most importantly, within ALL of our hearts. In fact, the passage of this prohibitive law supports the tenets of CRT.

To believe otherwise is to deny our stained history and current events. Are we not able to give up the delusion of American perfection?

Until we, as individuals and a nation, admit and diagnose that the evils of multidirectional racism exist and treat and cure them and embrace and celebrate our differences and our diversity and use them in a synergistic and collaborative way in pluralism, we will never become the bright city of refuge on the hill that we and the world so desperately need for us as a culture to be.

It is such a shame that our legislators have led us into a blind alley of ignorance rather than toward a greater understanding through proper education and leadership.

Notwithstanding, however, I am confident that our sons and daughters will learn to embrace each other in a new and better way in the future, despite our misguided efforts in keeping them from doing so.

Even if our past were seemingly perfect, the attempt to preserve the past always results in stifling of the best in our future.

Therefore, let us utilize proper and enlightening education to embrace a brighter and better future rather than embrace the sins in the reality of our past."

Let us determine to walk together in this better way as brothers. If we can, we will improve education and sense of community and will learn to cherish our diversity.

PS:

A poem speaking of the need for diversity and tolerance:

SNOWFLAKES

Pure, white snowflakes

Gently falling, as angel hair,

From God's own hand,

From heaven above

To earth so fair.

Each unique,

Different size and shape,

Slowly drifting with divine purpose,

Falling as a soul into the heart of man,

Each, a new precious life to make.

Then growing and living

In the love of God and man,

Some days happy, some days sad,

Like mount and valley,

Day and night changing place.

All allowed by God in His love and grace.

But, Oh! How sad.

Some are evil with black, hard hearts.

As God's life gifts

They snatch away

With no more thought than the joy

Of warm spring day.

Away they go

In a whirlwind of hate;

Forever torn asunder,

Husband from wife,

Babe from mother,

Friend from friend,

Dignity from soul,

And finally hope taken in plunder.

Clinging to final morsels of faith,

One by one they meet their fate.

Martyred and burned,

Bodies no longer held in prison wire

Souls fly up to God as reformed snowflakes,

Ever higher and higher,

There to be received by angelic choirs.

Purged gray ash

Falls on prison guards,

Pricking black, hard souls,

Placing them behind walls of guilt.

There, awaiting trial and judgment

Of God and man,

Hanged and condemned to hell's dark pit.

Those left behind

Struggle to live on, and oh, so lean,

Chased by grief so black,

Ne'er even to be seen,

But even so felt in heart

As twisting dagger, oh so sharp.

Good and evil living

Side by side, and in all our hearts

You see,

Until God makes it right

In tomorrow's eternity.

In memory of holocaust victims,

May we never forget.

OF GLORIFICATION

"Beloved, now are we the sons of God, and it doth not yet appear what we shall be: but we know that, when he shall appear, we shall be like him; for we shall see him as he is."

1 John 3:2

We are aware of the doctrines of the Creation, sin, the fall and the curse, and likewise how God has redeemed man through the blood of Jesus and how this sacrifice, when acted upon personally, by faith, can bring individual salvation. Moreover, we have considered why God has allowed suffering, pain and evil to continue to exist today and how that is related to his primary will in this age of bringing as many lost souls into the Church as possible.

And lastly, we are cognizant of how He has made provision for our patience and peace and endurance in the face of life's trials, and that it is His will for the individual believer in this age and during his life to become ever more like Jesus in humility, obedience, service and sacrifice, the process of sanctification. Sanctification, which is becoming like Jesus, then prepares us for the next life.

We know we are joint heirs with God's Son, Jesus, and so we are joint heirs, not only of His glory but also of His suffering. The suffering of this present time is not worthy of being compared to the glory that shall be revealed in us, both today to the lost and later, in heaven or eternity.

This brings us to a set of rather obvious questions. First, why did God, who was and is and always shall be perfect in every way within Himself, create the universe with man in it and in dominion over it, knowing that man would sin and bring the curse upon it, with all the untold suffering? Why did He do this, knowing that it would finally require Him to send His own Son to die a horrible death on the cross and bear all the sin and suffering of the entire race, while isolated and separated from the Father? It certainly is very difficult for the human mind to fathom.

Likewise, what is the nature of the glory we shall possess in heaven? It will certainly be grand if it will make us forget all the suffering of the past—and it will! Now we see God and His ways as through a dark window; but when we are in heaven, we will see Him face to face in all His glory, and He will teach us His ways and purposes. We will know Him and His ways and His creation, even as well as He knows Himself, His Creation and as He knows us. This much we know we are promised, and certainly this much is a good start in glory!

Romans Chapter 8 tells us the Holy Spirit is a down payment on this promise. He is here to live within us and to comfort, guide and instruct us and through prayer to have the will of God worked out in our lives. One could surmise that this is a foreshadowing of the perfect peace we shall have in heaven, resting perfectly in God's will and in a perfect relationship with Him. The Holy Spirit is leading us toward this in our lives today and is our guide on the path of sanctification. In fact, both the Lord in the upper room and Paul in Romans 8 use the metaphor of the creation being in labor, as a mother in childbirth, in giving birth to God's majestic plan of glory for the church, the body and bride of His Son, Christ. The universe is the womb of the church and its glory.

Let's turn to Scripture for the answers.

In the beginning, God created man in his own image (Genesis 1:26) which, in part, would mean Adam was a triune being, as are we, like God with a spirit, a soul and a body. (1 Thessalonians 5:23 and Hebrews 4:12). The triune parts of God are, of course, the Father and the Holy Spirit and the physical part, Christ, who later via the incarnation was physically born as a man, the second Adam (Romans, Chapter 5), taking on man's nature. Jesus is fully God and fully man in the incarnation. In Genesis, Chapter 2, God formed Adam from the dust of the earth and then breathed His own Spirit into Him in order to bring him to life in His own image.

Adam was of God and like God before he fell.

Likewise, in Genesis, Chapter 2, we read of the nearly perfect (imperfect because Adam had no knowledge of the good and evil that existed beyond him and beyond time and space) fellowship that existed between God and Adam and Eve. Man was a companion and a delight to God, and God was a companion and a delight to man.

As we have seen when Adam sinned and fell, death and the curse came upon him and all creation. God, however, through redemption and salvation, has made regeneration of the spirit and sanctification of the soul and ultimate glorification of the body of man possible. Also, even though all men will die physically, spiritual death will not come upon God's children, and we will not be forever separated from God, but will live with Him in glory through eternity. That fellowship that existed between God and man will be restored and indeed be richer and fuller with redeemed man than it ever could be with created, unfallen man. Perhaps this is the reason for God's creation, the fall and finally redemption.

What are redeemed man's final state and nature (essence) and relationship with God to be?

Romans Chapter 8 states we are the adopted sons of God, heirs and joint heirs with His only begotten Son, Jesus. As such, we have access to

Him at his throne and may even address Him as a child would a loving father, calling Him, 'Daddy.'

He has given us his own righteousness (2 Corinthians 5:17-21). God, through Christ, has made us new creatures with His divine nature (later paragraph) and with His own righteousness.

We are kings and priests unto God serving under the office Of Christ and we shall rule and reign with Him (Revelation 1:6 and 5:12).

2 Peter 1:4 declares that we, God's children, are partakers of God's divine nature. That is to say, we are as God in His nature, which is mirrored by the fruits of the Spirit. The Greek word used for nature here is 'physis', which means: God's inherent qualities or from Strong's Greek Lexicon: "the sum of innate properties and powers by which one person differs from others, distinctive native peculiarities, natural characteristics."

Now let's examine intrinsic as in 'divine nature; from Your Dictionary: "Of or relating to the essential nature of a thing". We see Peter is going beyond speaking of the mere sharing of characteristics or qualities and means sharing of essence. This would be the essence of His character and qualities which He shares beyond the mere characteristics themselves but not including His ontological nature, which is that which defines the Father as 'I AM' thus being that which will always separate the Creator from the created.

The Church is the physical body of Christ and He is the head while we are the members. (1 Corinthians, Chapter 15, Romans, Chapter 12, Ephesians 1:22-23). The Church is also the bride of Christ and He the head and husband (Ephesians 5:23, Revelation, Chapters 21 and 22). And upon Christ's harvesting his Church from the world at the end of this age, there will occur in heaven a magnificent marriage between the Lamb, the bridegroom, and the Church—the bride. Christ will not only have paid a dowry for His bride with His blood, but also will have redeemed her from the wages of sin, the blackness of spiritual death; and He will adorn her in pure white linen. What a celebration it will be!

Moreover, Ephesians 5:30 states that as the church, we are members of His body, of His flesh and of His bones, i.e., we are physically consubstantial (although obviously separate, an inscrutable paradox) with Christ, the physical part of the Trinity and who, in turn, is consubstantial with the Father and the Holy Spirit. The Church is the body of God's Son, Christ, and Christ is the head and bridegroom of His bride, the Church.

What can we glean from all of this? Before the Creation, God was perfectly complete in every way and perfectly holy and just. But He desired companionship, which He initially found in the garden with Adam and Eve. Then Adam and Eve sinned (which God knew would happen out of their free will, as He did not wish the companionship of puppets or automatons, but of those who would freely choose to be His companions and worship Him), forever breaking the relationship. God so loved man that He, over centuries, patiently gave a system of laws and entered covenants with man, which culminated in giving His own Son on the cross for our redemption, reinstating and enlarging the relationship. After the Church Age, in which He adds redeemed souls to His new family, He will command Christ to harvest His Church from the world to live with Him as His companion in heaven, as He did with Adam and Eve in the garden.

But the new relationship will go well beyond mere companionship. It is God's plan based on the above Scriptures to make us His very children with His own righteousness and divine nature and to rule and reign under Him as kings and priests.

And finally, let's look at John 17: 21-23. Jesus is praying in the upper room that God makes the members of the Church one, as are Jesus and the Father, and that the Church be one with God and Christ. To be one goes beyond like-mindedness or sharing of qualities and, in its purest sense, means to be in perfect identity with or the same as. If the Church is to be one with God and Christ, it becomes quite evident that God's plan is to make the Church, in some marvelous, miraculous, and mysterious way, a part of Himself (one with Him) in order to complete

Himself and to make us His perfect companions. This involves sharing the essence of His nature (character), i.e., consubstantial with Him. Christ did not pray that we be like-minded with God or like God but that we be one with each other and Christ as Christ and God are one.

The miracle of the incarnation of Christ taking on man's nature begets the miracle of glorification, man taking on God's nature. This in no way whatsoever supplants God the Father as the supreme being of all reality as it is His own divine plan, accomplished by the sacrifice of His only begotten, the firstborn of a new race or family of beings (Romans 8:29).

He referred to the original Creation as being very good, and Christ (John17:23) now refers to this new relationship as being perfect. He also has referred to this new relationship as being glorious, the same glory which God gave to Christ. This is the same glory of which Paul speaks in Romans, Chapter 8, which makes the suffering of this present time vanish in comparison.

For us, the glory of heaven will be so much more than the mansions and streets of gold or even the rest and peace. This is related to the fact that we will be one with God and Christ and explore and rule and reign and govern over the universe forever more!

The final irony is that God, for His own purposes, and in making a redeemed man a part of Himself accomplishes that which Adam and Eve tried to accomplish in the flesh by eating the fruit of the tree of knowledge of good and evil, knowledge God keeps for Himself in His own divine prerogative, but which He now plans to share with His Son's bride, the Church.

For me, when I first realized the fullness of our salvation, in glorification, I gained a wholly new concept of whom I am in God- nothing less, by His will and gift, a part of His divine self as a member of the body of His Son.

We, the church, will rule and reign over the creation, like God omniscient and omnipresent and existing beyond time in an infinite number of dimensions, learning and governing within His perfect will.

This knowledge sets a new awareness of the Great Commission, does it not? The whole world needs to know of God's great plan for us: sharing in His glory and praising Him forever!

Does God Really Exist?

I want to pose the following important question: Does God Really Exist?

Someone who is a Christian recently asked me this question. You see, this person has had an emotionally difficult life and, at times, like us all, has not sensed the very near presence of our Father. I also asked the same question of another friend, an ethnic Jew who was raised in an Orthodox home. His response was a seemingly frustrated and confused, "No." I must admit in moments of trial and weakness, I have pondered the same question.

But my answer to the question is a resounding, "Yes, God definitely does exist!" His existence cannot be proven by the scientific method as He requires His children to believe in Him by faith—the substance of things hoped for but not seen, i.e., belief in God's existence and His salvation is a matter of the heart and soul not of intellectual cognition. "You ask me how I know He lives. He lives within my heart!"

First, take a look at the creation and its order. There is an obvious design and balance in the stuff of the universe: Matter and antimatter, mass and gravity, light and energy and matter. On Earth, there is a miraculous recipe in the balance of crucial elements without which life could not exist: Distance from the sun regarding temperature, the makeup of the atmosphere, the amount of water and of its physical properties allowing its three phases at critical temperatures, the tilt of its axis, allowing for seasons and seasonality over most of its surface and many more.

Consider the nature of electromagnetism, including visible light, which not only warms us but allows sight and transferring its energy to special chemicals in plants, which is the foundational building block of the planet's food chain.

For life to have spontaneously evolved, first there would have to have occurred an atomic evolution of hydrogen into carbon, oxygen and nitrogen and others. Then these elements would have had to self-arrange themselves into molecules of water and later, complex amino acids, proteins and nucleic acids. Further regulatory proteins are encoded by RNA and DNA, and, in turn, the latter depends on regulatory proteins for proper function. Which came first or how could they have spontaneously and simultaneously evolved? Lastly, even if any of these complex molecules did indeed evolve, how did they become packaged in a living cell capable of replication and reproduction? These initial questions on the beginning of life do not even get us close to understanding how man could have evolved without a purpose or plan, complete with the ability to reproduce his own kind, think, walk, love others and worship his Creator and explore the depths of His creation.

Next is the obvious interweaving of human history with the purposes of God. From the establishment of the Jewish race to the succession of secular kingdoms in the Middle East culminating in the Roman Empire with its Pax Romana into which Christ was born and in which Christianity spread and flourished and which was conquered, and which was transformed by Christianity and to the relocation of the Jewish race in modern Israel, God's hand and will are clearly visible. Bible prophecy has been totally accurate in portraying history in advance until now, and it will certainly be the same in the future.

Additionally, there is a beautiful synergy with and fulfillment of the Old Covenant with the New Covenant. The laws, prophesies and festivals of the Old do perfectly reflect and point to the New in every way. As Christ said, He came to fulfill the Old, not to destroy it.

Very important to me, I know in my own heart that my God is real and near. He was with me when my wife and son died and comforted me as He has at other trying times in my life. He has also been with me in times of joy, and I know He has spoken to me in my soul in inaudible ways, but understandable and useful and encouraging for me. Perhaps the most awesome and wonderful of these times was on the morning of my nearly fatal auto accident as I was sitting alone in my car contemplating death and overcome with fear. His Spirit spoke to me and brought to my mind the Twenty-Third Psalm, which I recited in my mind; and I could see Christ in my mind's eye seated at God's right hand forever interceding for me. I knew it made no difference whether I lived or died, as my relationship with Him in that moment was all that mattered. Nothing else, either good or bad, in my life was of any importance. I was in His presence and at total peace.

I have seen the miraculous changes brought forth by knowing God in the lives of many others, including the brave women at the Bethany House, and there is no way but by the grace of God that such change could ever be affected.

In the end, it is fairly easy for a reasonable person to see that God really does exist by observing His creation and His creatures, as enumerated above. He clearly has had an overarching purpose from eternity past, which He will finally bring to fruition in eternity future: that being to create a perfect companion for Himself and as a part of Himself, redeemed man and His own church the body and bride of His own Son, Jesus Christ. This is the best and only logical conclusion from the examination of the physical and spiritual evidence. Indeed, we can never prove God's existence, but we can believe and know it by faith in our hearts.

Yes!

God does exist!

And He has a plan for all of His creation and for you and me!

PS:

A poem on Knowing God:

The Face of God

Oh God! My Father!

I knew thee first in my mother's womb,

As there, by your love,

I was consumed.

As I burst forth

Into wondrous life,

Into my heart

Poured your purest light.

And e're there you are

With warm hand on me

As I long to be in You

For all eternity.

In ev'ry way

And in ev'ry day

I see your face

By your holy grace.

In sunrise and in sunset

With colors bright,

I see your face

In this silent sight.

In birth and in death
And in all between
I see your great grace
Into my heart glory gleam.

In mountain mighty
And in sea crest green,
I sense your glory
Into my heart, let it beam!

In the light of day
And in the dark of night,
Exists the plent'ous plan of your mind
And into my soul, let it shine.

Now I see your face
As through a dark glass,
But in that day, I will know
You fully in my heart at last.

As I look into your heart and soul
And know your love
To depths untold;
My heart will soar to rapturous heights
As I glory at that sumptuous sight.

OF CHURCH

During my life, the church has always been an anchor in both the good and bad times. I have attended many types of churches, large and small, city and rural, sedate and charismatic.

I was raised in a small Methodist church founded by my ancestors. I attended a Pentecostal, charismatic church with Melynda and with her at home, the Church of Eternal Grace and Peace.

Melynda's and Ruth's mother came with her sister and her husband as a teenager to Nashville in the 1930s, where they planted the First Assembly of God Church.

In the 1990s, I met RF, pastor of FBC in Clarksville, where after a few years we became members and involved in voluntary medical mission work in Brazil and China, as previously discussed. These were life-changing events for our entire family.

We, at one point, almost moved to Istanbul and later China as full-time missionaries, but it never quite worked out; nevertheless, we founded the Bethany House in the wake of that failure.

We have heard the organ play magnificently and powerfully at Notre Dame in Paris and shared the Lord's supper at St. Paul's in London and in a humble house church in China, all very special experiences.

I have memories of singing songs as a child and Sunday School under Miss Nobbie and others, and the congregation sing praise to God terribly off key. To this day, I still sing off key, and when I go too far or get too loud, Ruth puts her elbow in my ribs and rubs to shut me up; I get the message.

A very special church to us is FBC on Saint Simmons Island, Georgia, where we are both loved and love. Our special pastor and friend, FH, lives and attends there. He went with me to China twice and we had a great time. In the medical clinic, we one day led several people to Christ and promptly took them to the river for baptism the next day. FH and DL, our beloved missionary leader, led in these baptisms along with leaders in the local church.

Once, after a local service, the local pastors and leaders relished in asking spiritual questions of their American counterparts. FH fielded the questions, and finally he was asked to explain the nature of the Holy Trinity. He only had a few minutes to tackle a subject which could fill volumes, but he did a great job, and the Chinese were so very appreciative. We could feel the love and fellowship.

The church is, of course, the living body of Christ. During the Lord's Supper event in China, there were about 50 persons packed into a small hot, sultry room. The doors were closed, and windows drawn for security. There were local Chinese, others from Macau and we Americans. We did not speak the same human language, but we were in a special and palpable holy unity as we shared the body and blood of our Savior. We were in a sacred union, and there was not a dry eye in the house. The memory and warm glow lasts in my heart until this very day.

On one trip, my young doctor friend took us to his local city, where obviously almost no one had ever seen Occidentals before; we were a curiosity. His family was so hospitable and gracious. We stopped by the church, and our friend played hymns on the piano. His mother handed Ruth a hymnal, of course, in Chinese. Soon thereafter, Ruth was blessed when she noticed that she and her Chinese sister were harmoniously singing a familiar song in two different languages.

On our trips there were many events I will never forget, including eating octopus soup, hearing DL tell my awful 'pig with the wooden leg' joke in Chinese, and hearing a rooster crow in the kitchen at breakfast. The fowl to his loss later sacrificed his very life to become our lunch. Bless him.

We absolutely loved the local foot massages. They were so soothing and relaxing at the end of the day. GH, a local attorney, often went with us; and on one occasion, while the young lady was massaging his shoulders, noticed his hair was a little unusual. She reached up and tugged on the piece, and when it lifted off his head, she loudly yelped in startled fear and threw it across the room. The room erupted into hysterical laughter. I bet she never, ever did that again.

The church is, of course, spiritually speaking, the holy bride and body of Christ and thus is the body of people within it and not the buildings in which it often convenes.

It is said to have five functions: Evangelism of the lost, discipleship of the newly saved, fellowship of the body of believers, ministry for people in need, and worship together of our most holy and gracious God.

The church is, and has been, a big and essential part of my life, providing life and sustenance. I am a better person by being in my local churches and have been greatly blessed in the relationships there. I trust I've been a blessing to others at the same time.

PS:

A poem of friendship and fellowship:

Friendship Sublime

What is a friend,

Except one who upon the other can always depend?

And when, falls into midst of fiery depths,

Saves fellow there in velvety soft, white feathery net,

Sans even one selfish thought or regret?

And when, in heaven's dizzying heights,

Like eagle doth soar,

One flies with the other,

Minds and wills interwoven

Seeing vistas together

Ne'er yet trodden before.

Or on any mean, mundane kind of day,

Find fun in any silly, simple game to play;

Or just be there

To come and see,

And share a hot toddy tea

Or special smile with thee.

Some close to shore

And in harbor safe

The one would keep,

So that cragged rock and dangerous tide

Would never be threat or mortal surprise.

But the other, wiser friend,

With great joy and emotion

Sends freely to open sea

With sails full of the winds
Of discovery and exultation.

Sometimes from youth
And other times much later,
Any fast friend, no matter how or when,
Gift from God
Making life paths spent together
Oh, so much the straighter!

Not necessary to say I'm sorry,
But saying it nevertheless,
Since not doing so
Would be less than one's very best.

The game of life is not won
By money made or power acquired,
But much, much more
By the lives we touch
And the ones who touch ours.

Friendships are as snowflakes
Gently drifting down to Mother Earth,
Reflecting, touching, sharing,
Conspiring in life's grand mirth.

Like binary stars,

Held in place by God's own hand,

Forever orbiting round and round,

Ever moving t'word each other,

While ne'er meant to touch,

Yet fulfillment still to be found.

As in two old men on a park bench

Exchanging fond memories,

Slowly flowing from mind to lips,

Like mystical notes from musician flute crisp.

Dangling for a magic moment in shattered air,

No feeling in life which can even compare.

Unique friendship,

Gift of God, for God.

Console, enjoy, energize

From day to day

And feats not yet fathomed

To be completed along the way.

Essence escaping mere words

Beyond the power of thought,

Slipping into the sweet sublime,

Indescribable as beauty of rose

Slowly discerned petal by petal

O'er the timbres of time.

With only a few in life's long way,

Do we dare share such thoughts of mind and heart.

Thus, here in life, for the other,

Lifting and carrying on

As God does for all

On golden heavenly throne.

CONCLUSION

So, what are we to conclude from all this?

First, I offer the story of my own life, not as a perfect model by any means, but rather, as perhaps in the hope my unique story and journey with God and my fellow man serve as a model and inspiration for you, my readers and fellow pilgrims.

Let's look at this classic verse one more time.

"He has told you, O man, what is good; and what does the LORD require of you but to do justice, and to love kindness, and to walk humbly with your God?"

Our God is not speaking of salvation here but the imperative of justice, love, kindness and humility in our relationships with God and man.

If we want justice, we should act with justice.

If we crave love, mercy and kindness, we should shower love, mercy and kindness onto others.

If we want others to act in humility, we should do the same first.

It is the Golden Rule of life.

If we give away our lives, we will find a new and richer life.

For me, this principle is embedded in my life's purpose statement of using my God-given gifts to first enrich the lives of those around me, thus enriching my own life.

Further, as we saw from 2 Corinthians 9, our God searches over the earth for the faithful in order to make them fountains of His kingdom resources of all types to become blessings to others, not only those we know but even for those we don't yet know. The more we give, the more He gives us again to further give and bless.

When is the last time we shared the Gospel with someone and led them to Christ, the greatest gift and blessing of all?

When have we visited someone in prison, either a literal or metaphorical one, with comfort or the news of freedom?

When was the last time we fed the hungry?

One of the most personal and heartwarming stories of my medical career occurred one Sunday morning years ago when I was on call at the hospital. I was seeing an elderly woman who asked if I were T Carrigan's son?

"Yes," I replied.

"He was one of the kindest men I ever knew. My husband had died, and my children and I were in dire straits. He, on several occasions, just showed up with groceries and left them. I will never forget."

Nor now shall I!

I've already related how Melynda constantly practiced these precepts, actually a defining characteristic of her life. I cannot tell you how many times Ruth has told me of acts of kindness she has performed for the needy. Almost always, I have perceived her acts have demonstrated God's love for those she has served, leading to sincere expressions of gratitude and evangelistic opportunity.

Of course, the New Testament equivalent of this verse in Micah is the operation of the fruits of the Holy Spirit in our lives: Love, joy, peace, patience, kindness, goodness, faithfulness, gentleness, self-control.

Certainly, however; the only prescription for the spiritual and physical death of this life is the blood of Christ and the salvation it brings.

Justification, under the law, redemption from slavery of sin, thus bringing regeneration of our spirits are the first and immediate effects of salvation, restoring our sonship with God.

As we have discussed, the lifelong process of sanctification of our souls is one of becoming more like Christ in our lives every day, following the example of Christ Himself as in Philippians 2, the working out, or the perfecting of our salvation.

This, in turn, prepares us for living the infinite life in the eternity of heaven as a part of the body of Christ and ruling and reigning and exploring with Him the everlasting wonders of the creation.

This is what Paul proclaims in Philippians 3:

"I count everything as loss because of the surpassing worth of knowing Christ Jesus my Lord. For his sake I have suffered the loss of all things and count them as rubbish, in order that I may gain Christ and be found in him, not having a righteousness of my own that comes from the law, but that which comes through faith in Christ, the righteousness from God that depends on faith— that I may know him and the power of his resurrection, and may share his sufferings, becoming like him in his death, that by any means possible I may attain the resurrection from the dead. Not that I have already obtained this or am already perfect, but I press on to make it my own, because Christ Jesus has made me his own. Brothers, I do not consider that I have made it my own. But one thing I do: forgetting what lies behind and straining forward to what lies ahead, I press on toward the goal for the prize of the upward call of God in Christ Jesus. Let those of us who are mature think this way, and if in anything you think otherwise, God will reveal that also to you. Only let us hold true to what we have attained."

This life is a marathon striving for the prize of becoming like Christ, which we will perfectly attain in heaven, the final stage and complete perfection of our salvation, our glorification.

Does this not make the Great Commission a deep and abiding imperative for Every Christian?

Yes, it does!

For some Christians, our religion is something we do on Sunday mornings and as we want else wise. True Christianity, however, should become and be a deep abiding presence of Christ within us, completely changing our very essence and redefining who we are and our purpose in this life.

Romans 12: 1 and 2 then become the medicine from and gift of our lives in sacrifice to bring others into the Kingdom of God. If we want to please our Father, let us offer our very lives to Him.

Writing this book for you has become a blessing to me as I have remembered the beginnings, joys, tragedies and all the rest of the events and gifts of God in my life. I can certainly see His creative hand in it.

His will for me and my will have mysteriously, miraculously and marvelously worked in concert and made me who I am, hopefully more like Christ each and every day. Not that I have already obtained this or am already perfect, but I press on to make it my own, because Christ Jesus has made me his own.

He will also do the same for you and all those you bring to Him!

For me, this takes me back to the beginnings of my life and the strength of our oak tree and the sustaining power of the spring water, the personal symbols of God in my life.

Now for my final thought of opportunity and at the same time perhaps even warning: Pressing on "for the cause of the upward call of God in Christ Jesus" may very well, as Paul states, in our maturity, involve being called out of our zone of comfort, in which we may have lived for decades.

This may well be required as we wrestle with God and with our lifelong assumptions and beliefs, as did Jacob in becoming Israel.

Abram certainly was called to a similar test to leaving all he knew to become Abraham.

Saul endured a cataclysmic change in becoming Paul.

Peter, the comfortable Jewish fisherman who denied Christ, found the enlightenment and empowerment of God's Holy Spirit, which led him to cast aside all his old fears and beliefs in proclaiming Christ to the Roman gentiles in the house of Cornelius.

Our Lord Himself, in His humanity, proceeded through several life crises, especially in leaving glory and going to the cross for us. He thus became our Emanuel, Savior and High Priest.

Let us look more closely at Jacob's experience at Bethel, where he experienced the reality of God for the first time. Upon awakening from his vision, he declared, "Surely the Lord is in this place; and I did not know it." This realization came upon him only after leaving his previous set of knowledge, beliefs, and realities. This affirmation and declaration serve not only as a celebration of the past but also an anticipation of the future in our relationship with God.

At this point in my life, I feel the strong and sure pull of God taking me into a deeper and fuller knowledge and relationship with Him, which I cannot attain in my present situation but which has and will nevertheless serve as my firm foundation in 'holding true' to it and building upon it. Comfort with the old is the greatest enemy of becoming a new creature.

There surely is another place in my relationship with God in which I have not known or could even imagine He existed on this side of eternity. As my son David said, I must walk over God's bridge beyond my current horizons to find Him in this new place.

I now pray to join Him there wherever it may be, just as the butterfly emerges from its cocoon into a new life.

Blessings to you, my dear reader, as you travel over your own bridges toward God.

PS:

I close with two poems looking into eternity:

Chrysalis

Man.

Created by God,

Made of His glory,

Bound for perfected, eternal grandeur,

But warped by sin,

Thus, wrapped in mortal flesh.

To be imprisoned there forever more?

No!

Saved by God,

By sending His own Son

From His glory,

Becoming our flesh,

Wrapped in the chrysalis of death,

But bursting forth in life forever more!

Yes!

Just as larva doomed for death

Sheds its mortal, fleshly coat

And from caterpillar

To wondrous butterfly doth molt,

Death begets glory
As He by His plan had sought.

Thus,
Nay, much more than molt,
Trading mortal flesh
For eternal glory
Foreshadowed by the Chrysalis of Christ
Carried 'cross that last Chrysalis crisis
None other than in tomb of God's own hands.

Now!
Worm to beautiful butterfly,
By Christ's own travail,
Death to death,
Glory to perfected glory,
God's own plan,
For our wondrous story!!

Just so,
Are human relationships not the same?
Peaks and valleys,
Chrysalis crises of another sort?
Lost days re-found?
Lost friends redeemed?
All according to what we dare dream?

All the same,

Souls, days, lives, friends

Passing from glory to glory,

Leaving chrysalis of death behind,

Cast aside as old worn cloak

Bursting forth as day's new dawn

Praising God anon and all along!

Frozen Moments

Life's stream thorough our souls does flow

Moment by moment

Day by day

E'er in our minds to stay.

Some come and go

Like the warm spring sun,

As they pass in peace

And warm hearts with joy and myrrh.

Others float as from a soft spring

Or mirrored from pale moon.

On cool, thin, wispy cloud

Refreshing the soul.

Many just go by unnoticed or unwanted,

Neglected by distraction,

Forever confined in the dust bin

Of the forgotten.

Others pierce the soul

As a hot burning summer furnace

Creating sandy dry desert bars

From which we yearn to escape.

Finally the crashing water falls,

Thrusting through our being

As long, sharp icicles of pain

Impaling on cragged, cold rock.

Never forgotten moments

Frozen forever in the mind,

A dangling memory

Mindful of fragility and mortality.

All sent from God

From eternity, into eternity

To shape and mold us

Into the likeness of His Son.

Then healing and cleansing

With the tide of heaven's flood

Sweeping us into His heart

There to abide forever.